What people say about Business Plan In A

❝A business plan is something every business needs, but too many fail to create one because it seems intimidating. Rhonda Abrams is on a mission to change that. With this book she shows you how to create a professional business plan that will seem like it took weeks to write instead of 24 hours.❞

— *Anita Campbell, Publisher of Small Business Trends*

❝I'm growing my business this year by purchasing a commercial building, and I needed a real estate loan to make the purchase. *Business Plan In A Day* was THE source I used for writing my plan, and the bankers and brokers I spoke with all commended my plan as being very strong and well-written. Thanks to you, I've secured my loan and the transaction is going through. I feel so fortunate to have found this book.❞

— *Lisa Stillman, Garden Walk Massage Therapy, St. Louis, MO*

Excellent for a comprehensive plan that is simple to do

❝We used this book in our seminar for our management staff in creating a Business Plan for their area of responsibility. Chief advantage was it makes you think in depth and present in a simple manner. Everyone enjoyed doing it and we now review annually.❞

— *Amazon*

Excellent tool!

❝Rhonda Abrams' book is an excellent tool for any entrepreneur. It is very well organized and simplifies the process. She has great insight and thoughtful suggestions. She includes many insider tips and where to find research data. This book is highly recommended.❞

— *Amazon*

The Book that Makes Business Planning Really Simple

❝Buy this book and follow it front to back. Go to the author's website and see other materials that she has on business planning. The best source there is.❞

— *Amazon*

A good day's planning

❝I hate business planning—but I had to do one. Thankfully, I found "Business Plan in a Day." It made the process almost fun—and I learned more about what I was trying to do with my business than I ever expected. The graphics helped and the sample components helped me clearly understand what I needed to write. For me as an unsophisticated business planner, this book was tremendously helpful.❞

— *Amazon*

good book

❝This is a great book. It is great to have an author get to the point quickly and effectively. Thank you for putting this book out there.❞

— *Amazon*

highly, highly recommend

❝If you need a business plan framework, this is the book that you need. Well organized and makes it simple.❞

— *Amazon*

❝This is the third book I've read on business plans, and it's simultaneously the most concise, most clearly written, and best at giving an overall picture of the process. There were several points that were not addressed in the other books I read.❞

— *Goodreads*

❝This is what you just need to start understanding and start working on your business plan for any project you have in mind.❞

— *Goodreads*

Praise for Books from PlanningShop

PlanningShop

" PlanningShop has been invaluable to our organization. We use PlanningShop materials for our entrepreneur classes because the content is comprehensive and constantly updated. "

— *Ken Freeman, Director Small Business Development Center, Yuba Community College District*

Six-Week Startup: A Step-by-Step Program for Starting your Business, Making Money, and Achieving your Goals

I started...and opened in six-weeks!

" This is a great book for business beginners (and even those who are on their second or third time around). It walks you through the well suggested steps of getting started. If you follow the plan...you should realistically be able to "start" in 6-weeks. "

— *Amazon*

Very helpful

" This book really does what it promises. I went through each week/chapter writing down what Rhonda told me to. It all flowed together beautifully, and I am now almost ready to put my web site live and ready for sales. I also contacted SCORE and the SBA as per her recommendation, and have the added value of the counsel of hundreds of counselors who can speak specifically into my situation. I don't think there is anything else Rhonda could add to make this book a better choice for the virgin entrepeneur. Four thumbs up—two are from my SBA counselor! "

— *Amazon*

Entrepreneurship: A Real-World Approach

You CAN be an entrepreneur!

❝ This second edition of what was a good book to begin with has made enough changes to make it an excellent guide for those thinking about starting their own business. It begins with exploring what it means to be an entrepreneur, moves into and provides tools and strategies for developing and planning a business, takes the next step to create the internal operational framework to meet the needs of all stakeholders in the business, and then ends with some suggestions on how to grow the business even into a global market. Being filled with outstanding examples and scenarios, the book is easy to read, follow, and understand. There are pages of references, extra sources, and practical applications that will guide nearly every business idea into a potentially thriving enterprise. The price of the book is a bargain considering the wealth that is in its pages. ❞

—*Amazon*

Great Book for Beginners

❝ Great book insight and provides sections as to where to begin. Includes chapters on marketing, legal, naming your business and more. Great book! ❞

—*Amazon*

Bringing the Cloud Down to Earth

❝ No matter how you refer to it, working in the Cloud is a fundamental business practice these days and Abrams has done a terrific job of making this sometimes confusing subject relevant and practical for businesses of all shapes and sizes. ❞

— *John Jantsch, author of* Duct Tape Marketing *and* The Referral Engine

The SH*T's Hit the Fan... Now What?!

☆☆☆☆☆

A Positive Voice

Rhonda Abrams offers smart, insightful advice that is down to earth and in touch with our current times. She really understands how small business is the lifeblood of our economy, as well as its deeper connection to community and culture. She is equal parts advocate, advisor, & cheerleader—highly recommended.

—Amazon

❝ In this latest book Rhonda Abrams has confirmed once again why she is a respected thought leader on what makes small businesses work. Her passion, dedication, and commitment to helping businesses achieve success is evident in all that she does. Whether you are a start-up, a mature business, or someone who supports them—this book is essential reading to give you the knowledge, tools, and inspiration that you need to succeed. ❞

— *Isaac D. Kremer, Executive Director, Metuchen Downtown Alliance, Metuchen, New Jersey*

❝ Rhonda Abrams is a brilliant and impassioned advocate for American small business. When my friends and family's businesses were floundering to survive the pandemic, Rhonda's amazing podcast series covering the governments' loan programs, including Paycheck Protection Program (PPP), was a lifesaver…She quickly became our top source of information. Through her counsel several friends and family members received business-saving assistance. We can't thank Rhonda enough! ❞

—M. Davis, Atlanta, GA

Successful Marketing: Secrets & Strategies

❝ Successful Marketing encourages students to think through standard marketing concepts while applying them directly to their business idea. ❞

— *Meredith Carpenter, Entrepreneurship Instructor, Haywood Community College*

Successful Business Plan: Secrets & Strategies

Buy it now or miss a plethora of very useful knowledge

❝ Quite possibly the best book out there to give your plan the momentum to get it done and get it right! This book is worth more than its weight in gold. I was intimidated at first glance, but the content flows seamlessly and the worksheets are a fantastic planning tool, some of them can even be physical pieces of the business plan. I highly recommend to anyone serious about starting a business, get this book immediately, regardless of where you are at in your planning process and you'll be the next person writing a 5 star review. Get it done and get it right! ❞

—*Amazon*

Jam Packed with Secrets and Strategies—Don't Pass This Book Up!

❝ Ms. Abrams has done an excellent job of putting it all together and imparting concrete business wisdom. The book is up-to-date and a great resource for anyone in business be it a small or large business. She hit the nail on the head in the Financial section. She is correct in strongly asserted that you DON'T ignore your finances if you're having a bad month. I wish I had been taught from this book when I was in College! ❞

—*Amazon*

❝ [*Successful Business Plan* is] user-friendly and exhaustive…highly recommended. Abrams' book works because she tirelessly researched the subject. Most how-to books on entrepreneurship aren't worth a dime; among the thousands of small business titles, Abrams' [is an] exception. ❞

— *Forbes Magazine*

❝ There are plenty of decent business-plan guides out there, but Abrams' was a cut above the others I saw. *Successful Business Plan* won points with me because it was thorough and well organized, with handy worksheets and good quotes. Also, Abrams does a better job than most at explaining the business plan as a planning tool rather than a formulaic exercise. Well done. ❞

— *Inc. Magazine*

“ We are again using *Successful Business Plan* in my business honors course this semester. Must be working, as Penn State was just named (by Kaplan and *Newsweek* magazine) as the 'hottest school in the U.S. for student entrepreneurs!' ”

— *Greg Pierce, Penn State University*

“ *Successful Business Plan* enables my Entrepreneurship students at the University of Vermont to develop really great business plans. The book's easy-to-follow, step-by-step format makes preparing a plan logical and understandable. Over the years...several students have actually launched their businesses successfully. Our son used the book at St. Michael's College in Vermont to develop a plan for airport fitness centers, winning the school's annual business plan competition for business majors...with a hefty cash prize! His plan was so thorough, especially the financials, that he was flown to the West Coast to present his plan to a prospective buyer. The bottom line, there is no better road map to business plan success than *Successful Business Plan*! ”

— *David Kaufman, University of Vermont*

“ If you'd like something that goes beyond the mere construction of your plan and is more fun to use, try *Successful Business Plan: Secrets and Strategies,* by Rhonda Abrams...this book can take the pain out of the process. ”

— *"Small Business School," PBS television show*

“ *Successful Business Plan* is easy to follow and comprehensive. From the first chapter to the last, it guides you through the business planning process with a proven systematic approach. ”

— *Sean S. Murphy, Ernst & Young LLP*

“ As a 20 plus year veteran SBDC director, consultant and entrepreneur-ship instructor, I have assisted thousands of individuals and business owners through the planning process. Having reviewed tens of thousands of plans and critiquing hundreds of planning texts, programs and tools, *Successful Business Plan: Secrets & Strategies* remains my hands-down favorite text/workbook/ guide. The content and construction is comprehensive, practical and 'do-able' for the serious small business owner/entrepreneur. ”

— *David Gay, Illinois Small Business Development Center at College of DuPage*

“In my opinion, your book is the definitive guide for successful business plans. I particularly appreciate and recommend the use of the Flow-Through Financial worksheets. Each is a great device to illustrate the connection between the qualitative and quantitative elements of a plan.”

— *Gene Elliott, Business Consultant, New Mexico*

“I've been using and promoting *Successful Business Plan* since 1993, and it's great! I've taught business plan writing in several local SBDCs, as well as nationally, through the Neighborhood Reinvestment Training Institute. My course is designed and delivered around your book.”

— *Ransom S. Stafford, Business Consultant, Twin Cities, MN*

“One of the best books on business planning. The overall quality of this book is excellent, but three things make it stand out: First, it contains worksheets that walk you through the information gathering process. Fill them out, and even the financials—always the hardest part of a plan—will fall right into place. Second, it has a sample plan that reads like a real business plan, written by a real person for a real business. You can use much of the wording in your own plan. Third, it has tips from successful managers, leaders, and business owners, large and small. I was especially fascinated reading the tips from ex-49'er head coach Bill Walsh. You can't go wrong following his advice on planning and organizing!”

— *Economic Chamber of Macedonia*

“*Successful Business Plan* is thorough, well-organized, and a very useful tool for business planning and development. It's an excellent guide to the details involved with creating a solid, useful business plan.”

— *Jim Jindrick, The Institute of Electrical and Electronics Engineers and the University of Arizona*

“I chose *Successful Business Plan* because of its ease of use, its clarity, and its good examples. I have used the book for a number of years now.”

— *Jean Morris, The Culinary Institute of America*

“It has a clearly defined, comprehensive approach.”

— *Zane Swanson, Emporia State University, KS*

PlanningShop
Palo Alto, California

BUSINESS PLAN

In A Day

4th Edition

**A complete business plan
in 24 hours or less!**

Rhonda Abrams

Business Plan In A Day, 4th Edition

© 2021 by Rhonda Abrams

Published by PlanningShop

SERVICES FOR OUR READERS:

Colleges, business schools, corporate purchasing:
PlanningShop™ offers special discounts and supplemental teaching materials for universities, business schools, and corporate training.

Contact: info@planningshop.com or call 650-364-9120.

FREE BUSINESS TIPS AND INFORMATION:

To receive PlanningShop's free email newsletter on starting and growing a successful business, sign up at www.PlanningShop.com.

PLANNINGSHOP:

555 Bryant Street, #180
Palo Alto, CA 94301 USA
650-364-9120
Fax: 650-364-9125
Email: info@PlanningShop.com
www.PlanningShop.com

PlanningShop is a division of Rhonda, Inc., a California corporation.

ACKNOWLEDGMENTS:

Editor: Anne Marie Bonneau
Cover and interior design: Arthur Wait; Diana Russell, www.DianaRussellDesign.com
Copyeditor: Emily Pickard
Indexing: Theresa Duran
Rhonda Abrams's photos: cover, Garrett Hubbard; page vii, Christopher Briscoe

ISBN 13: 978-1-933895-86-4 (print)
ISBN 13: 978-1-933895-89-5 (ebook)
Library of Congress Control Number: 2021930117

"This publication is designed to provide accurate and authoritative information in regard to the subject matter covered. It is sold with the understanding that the publisher and author are not engaged in rendering legal, accounting, or other professional services. If legal advice or other expert assistance is required, the services of a competent professional person should be sought."

— *from a Declaration of Principles jointly adopted by a committee of the American Bar Association and a committee of publishers.*

Printed in the United States of America

10 9 8 7 6 5 4 3 2 1

About the Author

Entrepreneur, author, and nationally syndicated columnist **Rhonda Abrams** is widely recognized as a leading expert on entrepreneurship and small business. Rhonda's column for *USA Today*, "Successful Strategies," is the most widely distributed column on small business and entrepreneurship in the United States, reaching tens of millions of readers each. She was named one of the "Top 30 Global Gurus" for Startups.

Rhonda's books have been used by millions of entrepreneurs. Her first book, *Successful Business Plan: Secrets & Strategies*, is the best-selling business plan guide in America and has sold over 2 million copies. It was named one of the Top Ten business books for entrepreneurs by both Forbes and *Inc.* magazines, and one of the 100 best business strategy books of all time. Rhonda's other books are perennial best sellers, with three of them having reached the nationally recognized "Top 50 Business Best-Seller" list.

Rhonda not only writes about business—she lives it! As the founder of three successful companies, Rhonda has accumulated an extraordinary depth of experience and a real-life understanding of the challenges facing entrepreneurs. Rhonda first founded a management consulting practice working with clients ranging from one-person startups to Fortune 500 companies. An early web pioneer, she founded a website for small business that she later sold. Today, Rhonda is CEO of the publishing company PlanningShop, which focuses exclusively on the topics of business planning, entrepreneurship, and new business development. PlanningShop is America's leading academic publisher in the discipline of entrepreneurship.

A popular public speaker, Rhonda regularly addresses leading industry and trade associations, business schools, and corporate conventions and events. Educated at Harvard University and UCLA, Rhonda lives in Palo Alto, California.

Rhonda Abrams:

 @RhondaAbramsSmallBusiness

 @RhondaAbrams

 @RhondaAbrams

The *In A Day* Promise
Get it done right, get it done fast!

You're busy. We can help.

PlanningShop is dedicated to helping entrepreneurs create and grow successful businesses. As entrepreneurs ourselves, we understand the many demands placed on you. We don't assume that you're a dummy, just that you're short on time.

This *In A Day* book will enable you to complete a critical business task in a hurry —and in the right way. You'll get it done right and get it done fast.

Can you complete this project in just twenty-four hours? Yes. Perhaps the twenty-four hours won't be consecutive. You may start—pause for an hour, day, or week to take care of other business—then return to the task later. Or, you may have some research or other preparation to do before you can complete this project.

We'll guide you through the process, show you what you absolutely have to do, and give you tips and tricks to help you reach your goals. We've talked to the experts and done the research so you don't have to. We've also eliminated any unnecessary steps so you don't waste your valuable time. That's the *In A Day* promise.

When you have a business task you need to do *now*, PlanningShop's *In A Day* books will help you get it done—in as little as a day.

Need a Business Plan Fast?

This Book Is for You!

You need a business plan—fast!

Maybe a potential investor has asked to see your plan by Tuesday. Perhaps you need a business plan to present at an upcoming staff meeting. Possibly you just want to get your business off the ground as quickly as possible.

Business Plan In A Day was created for busy people like you. This book delivers the critical, time-tested information and tools you need to develop a well-constructed and effective plan—quickly and efficiently.

Business Plan In A Day was designed to help you successfully achieve your goal. It's for people who need a business plan to:

- Seek financing from a bank or other lender
- Approach investors, such as angel investors or venture capitalists
- Create a new business

- Expand an existing business
- Report to management on department or team plans
- Set goals with, inform, and motivate team members or employees
- Enter a business plan competition or complete a college business plan project
- Plan the strategy and direction of a company

An effective business plan saves you time and money by focusing your business activities. It can give you control over your finances, marketing, and daily operations. A good plan can also help you raise the money you need to build your company. *Business Plan In A Day* gives you everything you need to get it done right—and get it done fast!

Want to learn more about business concepts and business plans?

For even more on business planning and business plans, see *Successful Business Plan*, available at bookstores or for online purchase at: **www.PlanningShop.com**.

Overview:
What's a Business Plan?

Your business plan is a powerful document telling the story of your company. It presents your current position, your vision for the future, and your plans for realizing that vision.

A business plan answers the following questions:

- What is your business idea or what is your existing business?

- Who are your existing and/or potential customers and what motivates them to buy from you?

- How will you let your customers know about your business?

- Who are your competitors and how are you different from them?

- How will you carry out the basic functions of your business?

- Is your management team capable of guiding your business to success?

- What is the long-range future of your business?

- What is your company's financial picture? How much money will it cost to run your business and how much money will you make?

Anatomy of a Business Plan

The basic parts of a complete business plan are:

- **Executive Summary:** Highlights the most important aspects of your business, summarizing key points of your business plan.

- **Company Description:** Features the basic, factual details about your business.

- **Target Market Description:** Identifies the types of people or businesses most likely to be your customers, and explains their needs and wants.

- **Competitive Analysis:** Evaluates other companies offering a similar product or service or filling a similar market need.

- **Marketing and Sales Plan:** Outlines how you will reach your customers and secure orders or make sales.

- **Operations Plan:** Explains how you run your business and the operational factors that may give you an edge over your competition.

- **Management Team:** Describes the key people running your business.

- **Development Plan and Milestones:** Shows where your business will be in several years' time, how you will get there, and the milestones you plan to reach along the way.

- **Financials:** A set of financial statements showing the current financial status and future financial goals of your company.

Although the Executive Summary appears first in your plan, prepare it last. You'll find it much easier to put together when you can draw from the highlights of each previously completed section.

Business Plan In A Day guides you quickly and efficiently through the process of developing a business plan. It's a roadmap to your success.

Time-Saving Tools

You probably already have a number of documents that will enable you to complete your plan faster. These include:

- Industry information, statistics, and data
- Surveys and other research about your target customers
- Information about your competition, including research from their websites
- Marketing brochures and other marketing materials
- Any past internal company planning papers
- Past tax returns (for existing companies)
- Organizational charts
- Charts depicting operational procedures
- Product data sheets

At the beginning of each step in this book, you'll find checklists showing the kinds of documents and other materials likely to provide helpful information for each section.

Contents

STEP 1: EXECUTIVE SUMMARY

Accomplishments

In this step you'll:

☐ Prepare your Executive Summary

Time-Saving Tools

You'll complete this section more quickly if you have any of the following handy:

☐ Information about your potential business plan readers
☐ Completed worksheets for Steps 2-9

Step 1

Executive Summary

Your Executive Summary is the single most important part of your business plan—particularly if you are seeking outside funding. Busy investors and lenders start reading here and use the Executive Summary to get an understanding of your business quickly.

In fact, some investors ask entrepreneurs to first send only their Executive Summary and financial statements (Step 9). If they like what they see, they'll request the full plan. So if you can hook your readers here, they'll ask for more. Your goal is both to summarize the major components of your business and to make your readers want to learn more.

This doesn't mean you can misrepresent your business. As in all parts of your business plan, the information and data you present in your Executive Summary must be truthful. But you can, and should, focus on those aspects of your business that show it in the very best light.

 **KEY TO SUCCESS**

First Things Last!

Even though your Executive Summary comes first in your business plan, you'll find it much easier to prepare—and much more compelling—if you write it last. Once you've completed the rest of your plan on the pages that follow, you'll find it much faster to come back and produce this section.

Your Executive Summary provides a *brief* snapshot of your business. Highlight the most important facts and concepts from your full business plan as concisely as possible. When completed, your Executive Summary will answer these questions for your readers:

- Does your basic concept make sense?
- Has your business been thoroughly planned?
- Is the management team capable?
- Is there a clear-cut market need for your product/service?
- What advantages do you have over your competition?
- Are your financial projections realistic?
- Is the business likely to succeed?
- Will investors be able to make money? Will lenders be able to get their money back?

Visualize your reader

As you create your Executive Summary, ask yourself, "Who's going to read my business plan?" You can improve your chances of getting a positive reaction if you keep your potential business plan reader in mind as you write.

Remember, your reader is only going to spend a few minutes on your Executive Summary. They're going to hone in on the issues that concern them most. If you understand their priorities, you'll be better able to craft it to push just the right buttons.

What Sets You Apart?

Think about the number of business plans your readers must plow through each day, especially if they're investors or bank lenders. (An average venture capitalist, for instance, usually sees about 1,000 plans a year.) What distinguishes yours from the rest of the stack? Early on in your Executive Summary, highlight the qualities that set you apart from all the other businesses. Put your winning concept up front and make sure your readers get it.

Do some homework to discover the interests and concerns of your likely business plan reader. Then put those issues near the top of your Executive Summary. A venture capitalist might want to see that you have groundbreaking new technology, and an angel investor might want to see that you've identified an easily reached target market, while a banker wants to know that the company owners are investing their own money in the business. Give more emphasis to those aspects that concern your reader most.

Of course, you might not be able to identify the particular person who's going to read your plan. In that case, you can focus on the *type* of person and their concerns. For instance, a banker is likely to look for aspects of your business plan that minimize risk, since they want to make sure their loan will be secure. An investor, on the other hand, looks for aspects that increase the chance that your company will grow large, since they will get a piece of the action. Refer to the interviews with investors and lenders in *The Experts Talk* on pages 168-182 to get a better idea of how each type of reader reviews business plans.

■ Prepare your summary

Your Executive Summary is the single most important part of your business plan. Readers will review it before they read any other section. Many readers will breeze through the Executive Summary, so you need to explain your business concept clearly, concisely, and in a way that makes them want to know more. Your Executive Summary is the first impression many readers will get of your company. Make sure it's a good one.

On pages 8-10, you'll find a worksheet to help you prepare your Executive Summary. Each question on the worksheet refers to corresponding worksheets throughout this book. You'll find it much easier—and quicker—to complete the Executive Summary worksheet if you've already worked through the rest of the steps in this book (Steps 2-9). Just refer to your completed worksheets to assemble the key ingredients for an informative, compelling Executive Summary.

Before you get to the worksheets, you'll see a sample Executive Summary for the fictional company ComputerEase. Review this model for more ideas about the content and structure of an Executive Summary.

KEY TO SUCCESS

Pay Attention to Preparation

A few ways to make your Executive Summary look appealing to readers:

- Divide the Summary into paragraphs that mirror the sections of your business plan.

- Keep each topic brief.

- Use bullets to highlight your most compelling information.

- Include a small chart or graph if it makes an important point clear.

- Use white space and informative subheads to break up text blocks and make the pages seem less intimidating.

For additional suggestions, see *Presentation Pointers* on pages 154-165.

SAMPLE PLAN:

Executive Summary

Immediately highlights a positive factor

THE COMPANY

ComputerEase, Incorporated, provides computer software and software-as-a-service (SaaS) training services, primarily to the corporate and business markets. In addition to offering local training at its own dedicated facilities, the firm delivers on-premises training to corporations located in the greater Vespucci, Indiana, area. It also offers online versions of its courses that can be accessed from anywhere with an Internet connection. The technology business services industry is one of the fastest growing in the United States, and ComputerEase intends to capitalize on that growth. The company's stock is currently held by President and CEO Charlotte Alexander and Ishaan Permaul, Vice President, Marketing.

Provides basic company details in a straightforward style

PRODUCTS AND SERVICES

The company provides software training programs targeted to the corporate market, and currently has a portfolio that covers a broad range of leading business software programs. There are two ways that training is delivered. On-premise training is provided by in-person instructors, either at the customer's place of business or at ComputerEase's Corporate Training Center. Online training is offered via the Internet. In addition to providing training for the most-used enterprise and business software and web-based business services, ComputerEase also creates custom programs at corporate customers' request for both on-premise and online delivery. The online training programs incorporate at least some video training segments, enhancing the learning experience.

Briefly describes the company's offerings

TARGET MARKETS

ComputerEase's "brick-and-mortar" business operates in the greater Vespucci, Indiana, area. Vespucci is the sixteenth-largest city in the United States, with a diverse and healthy economy. U.S. Census Bureau data show that more than 10,000 organizations with more than 50 employees (ComputerEase's primary target market) are located in the area. ComputerEase's online market is composed of English-speaking countries where a high percentage of businesses are automated or in the process of becoming automated. The market for online computer training has grown by more than 20 percent each year for the past five years, and is projected to sustain this rate of expansion for the remainder of the decade.

Shows large market potential

THE COMPETITION

No market leaders have yet emerged in the corporate software training field—either in the Vespucci region, or online. Competition is diverse and uneven, creating substantial market opportunities. ComputerEase maintains the following advantages over existing competition: strategic partnerships with leading software publishers; formal certifications from those publishers; a growing reputation for delivering highly effective training and superior customer support; a company-owned, state-of-the-art computer training center; a local sales staff with strong ties to target customers; and a national network of third-party consultants and computer retailers that bundle ComputerEase's courses with their own services.

Describes competitive edge

MARKETING AND SALES STRATEGY

ComputerEase differentiates itself in its marketing by emphasizing the needs of the corporation, not merely the students taking the classes. Locally, the firm employs highly regarded sales professionals with extensive ties to the target market who secure sales predominantly through face-to-face solicitations. For customers who access ComputerEase's online training, the company has an aggressive online marketing strategy that includes advertising on prominent training websites, exhibiting at training industry trade shows, publishing a monthly email newsletter on best practices in corporate training, and using search engine marketing by purchasing keywords. To support its customer base, ComputerEase also maintains an active Facebook business page, a LinkedIn profile, and a YouTube channel.

OPERATIONS

ComputerEase owns its Corporate Training Center with 20 PCs fully equipped with all the latest versions of the most popular business software programs. The company offers corporate training sessions at the Center, as well as at local corporations' place of business. It plans to open a second Training Center with some of the funds currently being sought. ComputerEase utilizes the excess capacity of the Training Center by offering Saturday and evening classes to consumers. Additionally, ComputerEase has three development PCs for creating the interactive course content based on the instructor-led courses and documentation. All equipment is leased, resulting in lower capital expenses and ensuring the latest equipment at all times. All data center operations, including the server that hosts the online training applications and student data, are outsourced to a locally managed services provider. Video production is outsourced to a local company experienced in creating instructional videos.

MANAGEMENT

President and Founder Charlotte Alexander brings significant technology-related management experience to this position. Immediately before starting ComputerEase, Alexander served as regional vice president for Wait's Electronics Emporium, a large computer hardware and electronics retail chain. Previously, she was a sales representative for IBM. Vice President Ishaan Permaul brings direct experience in marketing to the target market from his prior position as assistant marketing director for AlwaysHere Health Care Plan, and sales experience as a sales representative for SpeakUp Dictation Equipment.

Highlights management's relevant experience

FUTURE DEVELOPMENT AND EXIT STRATEGY

In addition to expanding online operations, ComputerEase will consider franchising. The company will also increase the number of company-run locations, choosing major metropolitan areas. Online, the company's goal is to become a major player in the corporate software training market. It would be open to merging with or being acquired by another leading online training brand or an online university or for-profit educational institution.

FINANCIALS

The financial strategy of ComputerEase emphasizes reinvestment of income for growth during the first few years of operation, with the company reaching profitability within the next three years. Annual revenue projections for the current year are $466,000; for year two, $987,750; and for year three, $1,637,230.

FUNDS SOUGHT AND USES

The company is currently seeking $160,000 in investment financing. These funds will be used for expansion, primarily opening an additional Training Center, hiring new staff, and increasing marketing activities. Long-term plans are for the company to aggressively expand its online business; work with customers to develop interactive online custom training programs for employees; and either develop a franchise operation or expand to become a regional company-owned chain, adding at least one training location annually.

Provides specific numbers and uses of funds. Hints at exit opportunity

My Executive Summary

What is your business all about? What are its most compelling qualities? Answer the questions on this worksheet, summarizing conclusions you've reached in the worksheets in Steps 2-9 of this book. Organize the information in a way that most appeals to your target reader. Combine related topics if that improves the flow.

THE COMPANY

What are the basic details of your business? (See worksheets on pages 15 and 17.)

PRODUCTS AND SERVICES

What products or services do you offer or plan to offer? (See worksheet on page 21.)

TARGET MARKET

Who are your customers? (Include a summary of any market research results.)
(See worksheet on page 43.)

THE COMPETITION

Who are your competitors? How is the market currently divided? What gives your company its competitive edge? (See worksheet on page 60.)

_____

_____

_____

_____

_____

_____

MARKETING AND SALES STRATEGY

How will you market and sell your product? (See worksheet on page 76.)

_____

_____

_____

_____

_____

OPERATIONS

What are your most important operational features? (See worksheet on page 92.)

_____

_____

_____

_____

_____

MANAGEMENT

Who are your founders? Who are the key members of your management team and what are their qualifications? (See worksheet on page 106.)

_____

_____

_____

_____

_____

DEVELOPMENT

What is the company's current stage of development? What are your long-term goals? What are some of the milestones you've met or plan to meet? What is your potential exit strategy? (See worksheet on page 120.)

_____

_____

_____

_____

_____

_____

FINANCIALS

What are the expected financial highlights or performance of your company? What are your company's expected gross sales and net profits? (Use gross sales and net profit figures from the worksheets on pages 132-133.)

_____

_____

_____

_____

_____

_____

_____

FUNDS SOUGHT AND USES

How much money are you seeking, from what sources, and how will the money be used? (See worksheets on pages 25 and 147.)

_____

_____

_____

_____

_____

_____

_____

_____

2

Accomplishments

In this step you'll:

- ☐ List your company's name(s) and location(s)
- ☐ Provide information about your company's ownership and legal structure
- ☐ Describe your company's history, development stage, and milestones
- ☐ Describe your product(s) and service(s)
- ☐ Give an overview of your industry
- ☐ Explain how your company has been funded to date and how much money you are seeking
- ☐ Pulling it all together: Company Description

Time-Saving Tools

You'll complete this section more quickly if you have any of the following handy:

- ☐ Business license(s), incorporation papers, or other key business documents
- ☐ Legal and financial agreements
- ☐ Product or service descriptions
- ☐ Dates of key developments in your company's history
- ☐ Industry research data

Company Description

The Company Description provides the basic details about your business. While your Executive Summary creates a compelling case for why your business will succeed, the Company Description fills in the necessary specifics.

While much of this information seems—and is—mundane, providing these facts is the foundation of the picture you paint of your company. Completing this section should not be particularly time consuming or cumbersome; the goal is to quickly provide background information about your company's structure, ownership, and developments to date.

This section also provides a glimpse of what's going on in your industry. Offering an overview of your industry is especially important if it is going through significant changes or facing economic difficulties. You'll need to show you understand the challenges your business, as part of that industry, faces. Of course, if your industry is healthy and growing, you'll want to point out those positive trends.

QUICK**TIP**

Missing Info?

If you're just starting your business, don't worry if you lack some of the information necessary to complete each part of this step. For example, if you haven't yet legally incorporated, indicate your intention to do so and in which state or province.

■ Give your company name(s) and location(s)

In the introductory section of your company description, include the basic details you'd put on any business application or form.

To begin, provide all the names associated with your company. In many cases, the name of your company or corporation is not the same as the name(s) you use when doing business with the public. You may actually have a number of different names associated with your business, including:

- Your own name

- If incorporated, the corporation name

- A DBA—or "doing business as"—also known as a "fictitious business name"

- Brand name(s)

- The name of your website

- Subsidiary companies

For instance, a restaurant called "Carla's Trattoria" might be legally owned by a corporation named C & J Food Enterprises. "Carla's Trattoria" is the DBA of the company, and both names should be listed in the business plan. If the restaurant's owners also bottle and sell spaghetti sauce, the name of the brand of their bottled foods ("Carla's Special Sauces") should also be listed.

List the location of your company's main place of business, any branch locations, and any other locations, such as warehouses. If you operate more than two or three branches, you can list the total number of locations here, but include a complete list of addresses in your business plan's Appendix.

SAMPLE PLAN:

Company Name and Location

ComputerEase, Inc., is an Indiana-based company providing computer software training services—both on-premises in the greater Vespucci, Indiana, area, and online—to business customers. It operates under the name "ComputerEase."

Name(s) of business

Corporate headquarters and the company's software training classroom are located at 987 South Main Street, Vespucci, Indiana. ComputerEase also offers software training classes at its corporate clients' offices.

Company address and location where they conduct business

What are the names associated with your company? (List all company names, including the legal name of the corporation, "DBA," brand or product names, names of subsidiaries, and domain names.)

Where is the company's main place of business? (Give the specific address, if known, or the general area or city if a location is yet to be selected.)

Do you have more than one location? (If so, list the address of each. If the company has many locations, list the total number and addresses or areas where they're located.)

■ Provide information about your company's ownership and legal status

Who owns your company? If yours is a one-person business, the answer may be simple: you do. But if you have gone into business with others, spell out the ownership division.

It's also important to specify the legal form of your business. Funders want to know what type of entity they're doing business with. Many businesses often start out as one form of business (such as sole proprietor) and incorporate later.

Other legal considerations to note here include:

- Licensing and distribution agreements

- Trademarks, copyrights, and patents

- Other legal protections you have secured to protect your proprietary business assets

- Other legal issues having a major impact on your business

What's Your Legal Status?

Sole Proprietorship: The company is not incorporated and is owned and managed by one person.

Partnership: Two or more people own the company, sharing profits, losses, and, usually, management. A legal partnership can exist even if you haven't drawn up legal partnership documents.

C Corporation: A corporate form that allows a large number and diversity of shareholders. Corporate income is taxed before profits or losses are distributed to shareholders.

S Corporation: A small corporation limited in the number and type of shareholders. It provides the liability protection of a C Corporation, but profits and losses are "passed through" to the owners' personal tax returns.

Limited Liability Company (LLC) or Limited Liability Partnership (LLP): A legal form of business offering benefits similar to those of an S Corporation but often with less cost and paperwork.

B Corporation: A type of corporation, allowed for in a few states, that is organized for the public benefit as well as for the benefit of the shareholders.

Not-for-Profit: An organization, agency, institution, charity, or company with charitable, educational, or other public benefit goals, that has been certified as tax exempt by the IRS.

SAMPLE PLAN:

Ownership and Legal Status

Status as a corporate entity

ComputerEase was incorporated in the state of Indiana one year ago. Ten thousand shares in the company have been issued: 6,000 are owned by President and CEO Charlotte Alexander; 1,000 are owned by Vice President of Marketing Ishaan Permaul; and 3,000 shares have been retained by the company for future distribution.

Indicates percent of ownership by each owner

The company was granted the trademark "ComputerEase" by the U.S. Patent and Trademark Office.

Another important legal consideration

What is the legal form of your business? (Sole proprietorship? Partnership? C Corporation? S Corporation? LLC? B Corporation?) **If it is incorporated, in which state or province?**

_____

_____

_____

Who owns your company? If the company has more than one owner, what percentage of the company does each own? If the company is incorporated, who owns the stock and in what amounts?

_____

_____

_____

What trademarks, copyrights, or patents does the company hold?

_____

_____

_____

What other important legal issues affect the company? (Distribution or licensing agreements? Major lawsuits? Regulatory concerns?)

_____

_____

_____

■ Describe your company's history, development stage, and milestones

Your company's history and milestones may make up the bulk of the Company Description portion of your business plan. In this section, you present the history and progress of your company.

First, indicate which phase of development your business is in. The basic stages are:

- **Seed company.** The business concept is developed, but the product or service is not yet finalized. Not yet making sales.

- **Startup.** In the early stages of operation. Securing first customers.

- **Expanding.** Established company adding new products, services, or branches. Rapidly increasing sales growth.

- **Stable.** Established company with modest ongoing sales growth.

- **Retrenchment.** Consolidating or repositioning product lines. Little or no sales growth.

Next, indicate the progress you've already made. Even if yours is a new business, you've almost certainly reached key milestones, such as developing a product prototype, securing seed financing, or finding office space. Be sure to include development details that indicate you're off to a good start.

If your company is up and running, you already have some major accomplishments under your belt, such as reaching significant sales levels, securing major customers, or shipping products. Highlight these in this portion of your Company Description.

SAMPLE PLAN:

Company History, Milestones, and Development to Date

Historical info

Founded in January 2021 by Charlotte Alexander, ComputerEase began operation by providing software training at corporate customers' offices.

In March 2021, Ishaan Permaul became Vice President for Marketing. Mr. Permaul immediately began an extensive sales campaign, targeting 200 large companies in the Vespucci area.

Identifies key milestone

In August 2021, ComputerEase opened its software Training Center at its present location in downtown Vespucci, enabling the company to significantly expand its offerings.

Also in August 2021, ComputerEase released its first online training classes, accessible over the company's website. Site licenses were offered to larger corporations with more extensive ongoing training needs.

In its first nine months of operation, the company conducted 184 training programs, and secured ongoing training contracts with 11 primary target corporate customers in its local geographic area. And despite investing very little in marketing its online programs during the first two months offering them, ComputerEase acquired three national accounts.

Key milestones reached

When was your company founded?

How would you describe your current phase of development? (Seed? Startup? Expanding? Stable? Retrenchment?)

What are some of the highlights of your company's history? What milestones have you reached so far?

■ Identify your product(s) or service(s)

Identify the specific types of products or services you sell. If you have a large product line or offer many services, you don't need to list each one separately. Instead, list the general categories.

For example, if you're opening a new gardening center, you don't need to list all the specific plants and products you'll sell, just the general nature of your merchandise: "a full line of plants for the home gardener, garden tools, planters and containers, organic plant food and fertilizer, and a small selection of gardening books."

When describing a product or service, provide just enough detail to give a clear picture of what it is or does. Too much detail makes this section cumbersome for your readers.

However, if you're seeking financing for a new type of product or service, particularly one that is not immediately understandable to your readers, provide more information. A brief explanation of what you'll be making or doing is appropriate here. Reserve detailed descriptions of production processes for the Appendix of your business plan.

If you are changing the nature of your products or services, or plan to make changes in the future, describe the changes you anticipate. Explain why you plan to make the change—perhaps a new production method will result in cost savings—and how you expect your product or service line to differ over time.

SAMPLE PLAN:

Services

ComputerEase offers training classes for users of all leading business software programs. The company also devises customer training programs for corporate clients. ComputerEase's classes are targeted primarily to the corporate market. Training classes can be taken online, or on-site at the customers' offices or at ComputerEase's Training Center in downtown Vespucci. To fully leverage the company's investment in hardware and software, the company offers online training courses in markets throughout the U.S.

Range and nature of services provided

List your product(s) and/or service(s) and describe its (their) function(s).

Product/Service	What It Does

What plans, if any, do you have to change your products or services in the future?

QUICK**TIP**

Sniffing Out Industry Info

Researching industry trends enables you to provide facts supporting your claims for your company's potential success. Let's say you're opening a doggie day spa. This idea might raise investor eyebrows. You'll help overcome their skepticism by providing data showing the dramatic increase in spending on pets in recent years. Even more convincing are sales figures for pet clothing boutiques, doggie day care centers, and specialty pet-food stores.

■ Describe your industry

No business is an island. Every business, including yours, operates as part of a larger overall industry. Forces affecting your industry as a whole will inevitably affect your business, as well.

Every industry changes. Some changes come about because the customers for the products or services change. For instance, aging baby boomers provide new opportunities for industries serving retirees or the elderly. Other industry changes occur because of new technology, outsourcing or offshoring, or corporate mergers.

Make sure you address the major changes occurring in your industry. The Internet in particular had an enormously disruptive impact on many industries. This is not a bad thing: with change comes opportunity. Indicate how you're prepared to take advantage of these opportunities, and respond appropriately to any challenges you face.

Pay particular attention to your industry's recent economic health and rate of growth. When looking for financing, potential funding sources ask tougher questions if you're in a troubled or shrinking industry than if you're in a healthy, expanding one.

Industry Developments and Trends

Healthy industry growth

ComputerEase is well positioned to take advantage of the significant opportunities presented by the rapidly expanding market for computer-related business services. From 2015 to 2019, the industry grew in excess of 62 percent, compared to an overall GDP increase of approximately 2.2 percent during that period.

The computer software training industry is in a state of flux, with no market leaders, nationally known providers, or widely recognized accreditation programs. Individual software manufacturers do offer certification as trainers for their products, but this certification is yet to be standardized, and such certification is not always crucial for consumers.

The key to success in the industry is to develop a regionally recognized brand in conjunction with online services, as is currently the case with other business services, such as accounting or human resources. Regionally dominant training companies are able to earn revenues and build market share sufficient to sustain continued development of online courses and support the high overhead cost of equipment, skilled trainers and subject matter experts, and materials.

Strategic opportunity

The current lack of industry leadership represents an opportunity for ComputerEase to develop a strong regional as well as online presence.

In what industry (or industries) does your company operate? What types of businesses belong to this industry?

Is your industry growing? What's the rate of growth?

What trends in the industry—paying special attention to those fueled by the Internet and ecommerce—have created opportunities for you?

What challenges, if any, is your industry facing?

How do you plan to capitalize on these opportunities and/or overcome these challenges?

QUICK**TIP**

Invest in Yourself

Most lenders and investors want to see that the business owners have already made a significant personal financial investment in their own company. Many loan programs require owners to contribute a certain percent (often 20 percent) toward any funds sought. So make certain you highlight the amount of money—as well as the time and other resources—you've already committed to your company.

■ Explain your company's funding

The purpose of this section is to provide a brief explanation of your financing to date and, if you're seeking financing, to describe how much money you need and for what purposes. It's not meant to provide a total financial picture of your company. That will be seen later in your financial statements.

Don't go into specific details, such as your accounts receivable or payable, here. However, indicate any major sources of future funds already committed to you. For instance, if you have secured a three-year contract with a large customer that will generate significant annual income, this is a good place to highlight that fact.

If you're using your business plan to seek financing, indicate how much money you're looking for and how you plan to use the money you receive. You'll expand on this in your "Sources and Use of Funds" worksheet on page 147.

GO GLOBAL:
International Industry Trends

Because of the global nature of business today, you need to consider not only industry trends in your own country, but industry trends worldwide. This is particularly true if you hope to sell your products or services internationally, but it is even true if you are sourcing materials or inventory worldwide, are using labor across national borders, or are hoping to take advantage of global industry advances to improve your own company's performance.

SAMPLE PLAN:

Funding to Date and Funds Sought

Indicates personal financial commitment of owner

Funding of the company to date has come from the personal savings of Ms. Alexander. This has amounted to a $60,000 investment and $40,000 in loans. In addition, the company has received a $30,000 loan from Ms. Alexander's family members. All other funding has come from the income generated by sales.

The company is now seeking $160,000 from outside investors. These funds will be used to open an additional Training Center, hire trainers, add staff, and expand marketing activities, especially for online courses.

Planned use of additional financing

How has the company been funded to date? How much have the company owners invested?

Has the company received funding from any other sources? If so, how much and on what terms?

What other major sources of funds has the company had?

How much money is the company seeking now and for what purposes?

The "Elevator Pitch"

In addition to the company description you'll include in your business plan, you'll also need to prepare an elevator pitch: a concise summary of your service, business, or product idea that can be delivered in one or two brief sentences. Before you attend your first networking event or trade show, approach a potential customer or investor, or speak with the press, you'll need to develop this.

The term "elevator pitch" is based on the premise that sometimes you can only catch an influential or powerful person for a few minutes—let's say in an elevator—and your pitch should be short enough for you to deliver it in the time it takes an elevator to go up a few floors. Since the typical elevator ride ranges from 30 to 60 seconds, keep your pitch to 100 to 150 words.

A good elevator pitch offers the following information:

- **What your business makes or does.** This should be very brief: "My company manufactures water- and weather-proof, solar-powered outdoor lights."

- **What market you serve.** You should be very specific about this: "Males between the ages of 15 and 30 who daily play video games" or "Small businesses with five to 10 employees."

- **How you plan to make money.** Because investors will want to know how you will earn a profit, when pitching to them, you need to be very explicit about the business model you plan to employ. For example, "We will charge a monthly subscription ranging from $5 to $25 per user."

- **How your business compares to other, familiar businesses.** If you compare your business to other similar businesses, people may more easily understand what your product or service is all about. For example, a new social networking site for lawyers might be described as "Like Facebook for law-firm employees."

- **Why you will succeed.** What market conditions will make your idea a surefire success? You need to use all your powers of persuasion here. If you have hard numbers to back up your assertions, use them: "Census figures show that young families are moving into this area at a rapid pace (up 27% over the previous decade), and those families will require housing."

- **Your ultimate goals for the business.** Do you want to eventually run a multinational corporation, or do you want to keep it relatively small and contained? You should be prepared to articulate your vision for the business's size and reach.

An elevator pitch is essential to marketing. So work on it carefully and practice it until you remember it and can repeat it easily.

My Company:
_____

Named:
_____

Does:
_____

Serves Which Market:
_____

Makes Money By:
_____

Is Like What Other Companies:
_____

Will Succeed Because It:
_____

Aims to Achieve:
_____

Sample Elevator Pitch

ComputerEase trains individuals and employees of corporate clients in the leading business software programs and applications, whether based in the cloud or on-premise. We conduct our classes online nationally and in-person in the greater Vespucci area, in our Training Center or on the premises of our clients. Our training sessions run between $99 and $1000 per student. ComputerEase intends to take advantage of the absence of a clear market leader in the area of online software training, in order to become a major player in the field. Our cutting-edge and professionally developed teaching materials, extensive offerings of training programs, and experienced management and staff will enable us to seize a large piece of the growth opportunity in the online computer software and application training space.

■ Pulling it all together: Company Description

A concise Company Description serves as a clear and convenient summary of the basic details of your company. Your Company Description provides readers with the facts they need to know about your company before delving deeper into your plan.

Draw from the information you provided in the worksheets in this step to complete this final worksheet.

What is the name and location of your company? (See worksheet on page 15.)

_____

_____

Who owns the company and what is its legal status? (See worksheet on page 17.)

_____

What is your company's current phase of development, and what milestones have you reached to date? (See worksheet on page 19.)

_____

_____

_____

What products and/or services do you offer? (See worksheet on page 21.)

_____

_____

What is the current health of your industry and what are the key trends? (See worksheet on page 23.)

_____

_____

_____

How has your company been funded to date? If you're looking for financing, how much money are you seeking and for what purposes? (See worksheet on page 25.)

_____

_____

_____

3

Accomplishments

In this step you'll:

- ☐ Specify the geographic location and reach of your target market area
- ☐ Describe the demographic characteristics of your customers
- ☐ Explain customer motivations and needs
- ☐ Determine the size of your market
- ☐ Evaluate market trends
- ☐ Pulling it all together: Target Market

Time-Saving Tools

You'll complete this section more quickly if you have any of the following handy:

- ☐ Maps of your target market area if you have a brick-and-mortar business
- ☐ Customer surveys
- ☐ Market research reports
- ☐ Industry research indicating market trends
- ☐ Books, magazines, and other media geared toward your target market
- ☐ Census data showing customer demographics

Step 3

Target Market

Your success rides on your ability to meet the needs and desires of your customers. In Step 3, identify these customers—not the *specific* people or businesses, but the *types* of customers you expect to serve. This is your target market.

Your goal is to assure readers of your Business Plan that:

- These customers do exist

- You know exactly who they are and what they want

- There are enough of them to support your business

- They're ready for what you have to offer and will actually buy

Paint a clear and detailed portrait of your customers— who they are, where they're located, how they think, why they buy, and what they want. This makes it easier to show how you plan to respond to their needs.

Strong target market definitions are based on observable characteristics, backed by data and research. This section outlines the kinds of information to include in a convincing target market description. See tips on collecting market research data on pages 32-33. If you have already done some market research, you'll complete this section more quickly.

KEY TO SUCCESS

Creating a Credible Market Definition

A strong target market definition is:

- **Definable.** It identifies the specific characteristics potential customers have in common.

- **Meaningful.** These characteristics directly relate to purchasing decisions.

- **Sizable.** The number of those potential customers is large enough to sustain your business.

- **Reachable.** You can affordably and effectively market to them.

■ Specify the geographic location and reach of your target market

Provide details about the geographic location you're planning to serve. On the worksheet opposite, show where your customers live or where their businesses operate. Explain how other characteristics about the location affect your customers and your business.

If relevant to your business, include such information as:

- Neighborhood, city, state, province, region, country, or international region

- Density of the area (urban, suburban, or rural)

- Climate (hot weather, cold weather, sunny, rainy, snowy)

- Traffic patterns (busy intersection, pedestrian area)

At this point, you are simply describing your target market geographic area, but your ultimate goal is to show the impact of its location on your business, if any.

If you're planning to sell some or all of your goods and services online, the geographic location of your business is much less critical. Literally, the world is your market. But don't just issue a blanket statement to that effect. Issues like fulfillment (if you are selling a physical product), language barriers (if you are selling a service), customs and import/export regulations, and differences in market demand will limit your reach. For instance, if you sell parkas online, you probably won't get too many orders from Tahiti! Likewise, an offer of English-to-French translation services will probably not find many buyers in Latin America.

SAMPLE PLAN:

Target Market Location

ComputerEase operates in the greater Vespucci, Indiana, area. Online, the target geographic market location includes the English-speaking countries with high levels of business automation. In person, the geographic area includes the incorporated cities of:

- Vespucci
- Whitten Park
- Smithfield

And the suburban communities (with business centers) of:

- Karen's Springs
- Gaspar
- Lake Bonneau

Geographic description

What geographic area will your business serve? (City? Country? Region?)

_____

_____

_____

_____

_____

What type of area is it? (Urban? Rural? Suburban?) **What's the population density?**

_____

_____

_____

_____

_____

What are some other details related to the area your business will serve?
(Climate conditions? Traffic patterns?)

_____

_____

_____

_____

Conducting Market Research

Get to know your customers or potential customers. Try these tips to gain insight into your customers' needs and desires and to gather data that support your assumptions about your target market:

- Talk to people or businesses that are, or could be, your customers. Ask them about what they want and need as related to your business.

- Conduct surveys and focus groups. These can be as informal as going to a mall and asking questions of consumers. If your budget allows, hire a professional market research firm to conduct interviews, or use an online survey tool.

- Examine the media that your customers read, listen to, or view. Most media outlets, including newspapers, magazines, and radio and television stations, keep detailed demographic profiles of their audience and know what interests them.

- Check the websites and social media platforms your customers visit, especially those in which they share their views.

- Check your local library. Your librarian can point you to online databases and print resources that provide data on your customers.

- Pay a visit (or several visits) to your competitors' places of business. Check out their websites and social media profiles. Figure out what they do to attract and serve customers.

Get a Media Kit

Media outlets—magazines and newspapers, radio and TV stations—can be a good source of demographic and lifestyle info about their audiences. If you know your target customers are likely to read a particular magazine, call the publication and request an advertiser or media kit. Chances are, it will include demographic data you can use. Some publications put these kits right on their websites. (Follow the links for advertisers, often found in the "About Us" section.)

Getting the Dirt on Your Market

Ever wonder why there seem to be three or four fast-food joints at the same intersection? Or why, all of a sudden, not one but three office-supply stores open in the same community?

The answer is that they all rely on similar statistics to choose locations. They look for particular factors: population density, characteristics of nearby residents (such as age, gender, income), and number and type of existing local businesses. You can see this same "clustering" of like businesses online. If a need exists, it will probably be identified by one or more of the multitude of industry-specific market research studies being published on a daily basis. Once such an identification is made, you can bet that a number of enterprising entrepreneurs will spring into action to meet it.

Big corporations hire consulting firms to compile these statistics. You've got an even bigger consulting group doing it for you—free! The United States government, particularly the Census Bureau, compiles a great deal of data useful for businesses, as does the Canadian government. You'll also find many international resources online.

A few key websites for finding market data:

- *www.census.gov:* U.S. Census Bureau. The entry page for all U.S. census data. Use this resource to access information about people, businesses, geography, trade, and much more.

- *https://www.census.gov/quickfacts/fact/table/US/PST045219:* QuickFacts. An easy-to-use website providing fast access to a wide variety of information about population characteristics at the state or county level.

- *www.statcan.gc.ca:* Statistics Canada. The entry page for data about Canada compiled by the Canadian government. Search by subject, such as "Families and households," "Income, pensions, spending and wealth," and "Population and demography," or search by key resource, such as "Data," "Analysis," or "Census."

- *www.worldbank.org:* This international organization compiles data worldwide. It offers free data by topic or country, contains links to online databases, and publishes its own economic reports.

QUICK**TIP**

Who's Your Customer?

Often, the person who purchases your product or service is not the same one who uses it. If you're selling to businesses, a purchasing department or supervisor may be the decision maker. If you're selling to consumers, a parent or spouse may be the decision maker and not the actual end user. You need to understand the needs and motivations of both the buyer and the ultimate end user.

■ Describe the demographic characteristics of your target customers

Discuss the observable, factual characteristics of your target customers—traits such as age, income level, family size, gender, and ethnic group. If you are targeting businesses rather than consumers, these characteristics would include traits such as which industries they're in, the size of the companies, and their stage of development (new business, expanding, or shrinking). Look for *meaningful* characteristics that directly relate to your customers' decisions to purchase.

Say you're opening an upscale hair salon in Manhattan. You identify your primary target customers as single, college-educated, professional women, aged 35-50, with annual income levels ranging from $90,000 to $160,000. These demographic details indicate this group has more money to spend on high-priced salon services and the motivation to spend it. Note that the difference between an on-premise establishment and an online business could be significant. For example, if you wanted to not only have a hair salon in Manhattan, but also sell your proprietary beauty supplies online, you might find that you can't charge as much for them online as you can in your brick-and-mortar establishment, as online shoppers are notoriously more price-sensitive. Your target customer might change as a result—say, a younger crowd that earns less annually, but spends more of its income on beauty products.

Using the worksheet opposite, fill in details on your target market. The more specific your details, the more credible your market definition.

SAMPLE PLAN:

Target Customer Characteristics

ComputerEase primarily targets large- and medium-size businesses with high computer use. They have:

- More than 50 employees
- High employee turnover
- An expanding number of employees
- A high dependence on computers

They are in the following industries:

- Government
- Insurance
- Financial/Banking
- Accounting
- Colleges and universities
- Engineering
- Hospitals and other medical facilities
- Airlines

Demographic and business-style characteristics

ComputerEase conducted a market research survey with a selection of targeted companies. It showed:

- 42% of these companies have a "training" amount allotted in their current year's budget.
- 18% specifically have "computer or software training" budgeted for the current year.
- 34% have purchased software training services in the last year.
- 66% indicated they would purchase more training than at present if better-quality, more-reliable training were available.
- 72% said they wanted to minimize the amount of time employees spent out of the office for training, and that they would pay a premium for online training that workers could complete without leaving their desks.

What are general, observable traits of your customers (especially those related to their likelihood of buying your product or service)?

Consumer (Age? Income range? Gender? Occupation? Marital status? Family size? Education level? Hobbies?)

Business (Industries? Years in business? Revenues? Number of employees? Specific business needs?)

■ Explain customer motivations and purchasing patterns

In addition to their observable demographic characteristics, highlight the less tangible, but no less real, factors influencing your customers' purchasing decisions. These include specific purchasing preferences, motivations based on how your customers view themselves, and how and when they actually buy.

When describing customer motivations, consider these questions:

- What concerns your customers most when making purchases? (Is it price? Quality? Convenience?)

- How quickly do they make their buying choices?

- Where do they usually buy their products or services?

- With what kinds of companies do they prefer to do business? (Large? Small? Socially responsible? Locally based?)

- How do your customers view themselves? (Do they see themselves as leading-edge? Technically savvy? Smart shoppers?)

When describing customer purchasing patterns, consider:

- Who makes the decision to purchase, if other than the end user?

- How often do they buy?

- How do they pay? (Cash? Credit? Purchase order? 30-, 60-, or 90-day terms?)

Assess the organizational factors involved, especially if you are selling to other businesses. For example, large companies typically have formalized procurement systems, leading to slow purchasing decisions. This will affect the length of your sales cycle.

SAMPLE PLAN:

Customer Motivations and Purchasing Patterns

In the corporations that ComputerEase targets, the decision to purchase computer software training is typically made by the human resources director or department. It often takes six to 12 months for a decision to be made. The critical issues influencing the decision are quality of the training, reliability, and responsiveness to specific corporate needs. Price is a consideration, but typically not the primary one.

Management personnel view themselves as responsible and professional. They prefer to deal with service companies that present a stable, professional image. They're often considerably influenced by the fact that similar companies already use the service or product.

Buying patterns

Customer motivations

Self-image issues

What factors most influence your customers' purchasing decisions?

Consumer (Price? Brand? Customer service? Features? Packaging? Return policy?)

Business (Price? Reputation/stability of service provider? Fast delivery?)

How do your customers view themselves?

Consumer (Trendsetter? Good housekeeper?)

Business (Industry leader? Fiscally prudent?)

How do your customers actually purchase your products or services? Who makes the purchasing decision? Where and how frequently do they purchase?

Consumer

Business

QUICK**TIP**

Numbers, Numbers, Numbers

Your business plan will be more convincing with solid numbers describing the size of your target market. When your numbers come from a reliable source, numerical data show you've done your homework. For U.S. companies, you'll find a surprisingly large amount of geographic and demographic data at the U.S. Census Bureau's website: *www.census.gov*.

■ Determine your market size

Is your market big enough to keep you in business? You want to make sure your pool of potential customers is large enough to sustain you. If you're looking for investors, you need to convince potential funders that your company can grow to a size that will make their investment profitable.

On the other hand, is your market so large you could never reach it affordably? If your market is too large, you probably have not defined its specific characteristics well enough to be able to design an effective and affordable marketing and sales process. Be realistic about the size of your market and your ability to serve it.

For some businesses, especially smaller ones, determining whether your market size is sufficient will be mostly a matter of intuition. But if yours is a bigger company, or if you're seeking investors, gather data to support your plan.

Be Specific

It's tempting to include just about everyone in the definition of your target market; after all, couldn't the whole world benefit from your product or service? Not only is this unrealistic, it makes it seem as if you haven't really zeroed in on who your real customers are—or could be. By detailing specific characteristics of your target market, you give readers a clearer view of your customers. Doing this will also save you time and money in future marketing efforts.

SAMPLE PLAN:

Market Size

The online market for computer training is large and growing exponentially as people have increasingly become accustomed to using—and relying upon—Web-based applications for more and more aspects of their lives, including education and training. Also, as companies automate more of their business processes, they require quick and efficient ways to get their employees up to date on new or upgraded business software—both off-the-shelf and specifically designed for their organizations. Vespucci and its surrounding communities make up a large and economically healthy area. According to census figures, the city of Vespucci has a population of approximately 775,000, making it the 18th-largest city in the U.S. The Vespucci Metropolitan Statistical Area (MSA) has an overall population approaching 1,500,000.

Market size data

The business climate has been consistently strong due to Vespucci's diverse economic base. The Vespucci MSA includes three county seats and is the home to numerous government offices.

The Vespucci Chamber of Commerce estimates that, of the more than 2,000 companies and institutions with more than 50 employees in the Greater Vespucci area, at least 1,500 are in the primary industries targeted by ComputerEase.

Also located in the Greater Vespucci area are:

Additional geographic information

- An international airport
- The regional processing centers for three national insurance companies
- The data processing center for the state's highway patrol
- A state university and six other colleges and universities
- A major medical center

What is the approximate size of your target market? (Include population of geographic area, if relevant, and total number of potential target customers.)

What other factors influence the size of the potential pool of customers?

■ Evaluate market trends

Change happens. You can't be a fortune-teller, but the most successful companies stay aware of trends that can affect their businesses. Such trends include: a growing (or shrinking) population, a hiring boom (or layoffs) in your area, a shift in the kinds of people or businesses populating the area, and new technologies. In this section, highlight the trends in your market, especially those that will have a positive impact on your business. Address trends that are occurring both in your geographic area and among the types of customers you serve.

Trade Associations

Trade associations are excellent sources of information about both the current customers in an industry and trends affecting that industry. Check with your industry's trade association for studies and forecasts they've published. You can find a list of trade associations at PlanningShop's website: **www.PlanningShop.com/associations**.

 ## GO GLOBAL:
Target Market

If you target international customers, be sure to outline the following information in your business plan:

- Countries served
- Population
- Targeted areas within country (cities, rural, suburban)
- Level of development (developed, emerging)
- Climate conditions
- Languages spoken
- Quality of infrastructure (e.g., roads, telecommunications, utilities)

SAMPLE PLAN:

Market Trends

The market for online training has grown by more than 20 percent annually over the last five years—a trend that is expected to continue for the rest of the decade. Even when the economy slows, demand for computer-based training accelerates, as it's by means of automation that companies increase worker productivity and reduce overall operating costs. The economic base of the Greater Vespucci area has been expanding. According to the Census Bureau, in the last four years the number of paid employees in the area has increased by over 5,000.
A survey by the local newspaper, the *Vespucci Explorer*, has shown that 43% of larger companies intend to add employees in the next 24 months.

Promising trends

What is the rate of growth of your target market?

What changes are occurring in the makeup of the market? (Include changes in technology, in the economy, and in social values and concerns.)

■ Pulling it all together: Target Market

A key part of creating your plan, and running your business, is understanding your customers—who they are, what they want, how they make their purchases. This information helps you more successfully design your products or services, develop your marketing, and secure sales.

Now that you're well acquainted with your target customers and their needs, pull together the highlights of your target market definition. Complete the worksheet below, choosing the most important and relevant information you've compiled in Step 3. You can reorder the information to highlight the most compelling aspects of your target market.

Where is your target market located? (See worksheet on page 33.)

_____

_____

What are the characteristics of your target customers? (See worksheet on page 37.)

_____

_____

What motivates your customers to make purchases and what are their buying patterns? (See worksheet on page 39.)

_____

_____

What is the size of your market? (See worksheet on page 41.)

_____

_____

What are some key market trends? (See worksheet on page 43.)

_____

_____

_____

Accomplishments

In this step you'll:

- [ ] Identify the types of competition you face
- [ ] List your specific competitors
- [ ] Determine market share distribution
- [ ] Analyze the strength of your competitors
- [ ] Highlight your competitive edge
- [ ] Evaluate the barriers to entry and potential competition
- [ ] Pulling it all together: The Competition

Time-Saving Tools

You'll complete this section more quickly if you have any of the following handy:

- [ ] A list of major competitors
- [ ] Research on your competitors
- [ ] Industry or trade journal articles

Step 4

The Competition

No matter what type of business you own or are planning to start, other companies want your customers. The fact that competition exists means you have tapped into a viable market with customers who wish to buy the goods or services you have to sell. That's why other businesses, like yours, want to profit from them.

Even if you are trying to sell a new type of product, such as a groundbreaking new technology, expect competition. There may be no comparable product on the market, but there's probably something else that fits the market need. Take Netflix, for instance. When the company started, it sent DVDs through the mail. This was quite innovative—DVDs were relatively new and no one was sending them through the mail. But competition still came from many sources. People could rent DVDs from video stores or record movies on their home video recorders.

The words "we have no competition" in a business plan indicate to potential investors that a) an entrepreneur hasn't fully examined the realities of the business, or b) no market exists for the concept. If you're sure you have a market, you can be sure you have competition.

 **KEY TO SUCCESS**

Understanding your competition proves you can:

- Distinguish your company from others

- Identify factors that will make customers choose your offerings over others

- Respond to needs that aren't currently being addressed by competitors

- Figure out what you're up against and be prepared to tackle competitive obstacles to your success

In the short term, understanding—and describing—your competition helps you present a stronger case to your business plan readers. In the long term, keeping an eye on your competition keeps you on your toes and helps you build and run a better business.

Just as important as *knowing* your competition is *learning* from it. Watch what your competitors are doing right and doing wrong. That will show you how to better serve your potential customers and uncover strategic opportunities in the market.

QUICK**TIP**

A strong competition section answers these questions:

- Who are your major competitors?

- On what basis do you compete? (Price? Convenience? Features? Service?)

- How do your offerings objectively compare to those of your competitors?

- How many new companies have entered the field in the past few years? Who are they?

- What barriers to entry make it difficult for new competitors to enter the market?

- What new competition might surface in the future?

■ Identify types of competition

What kinds of businesses contend with you for your customers' attention and dollars? Refer to *categories* of businesses here, rather than specific establishments. (You'll do that later.) For example, a clothing boutique might identify all similar boutiques within a 10-mile radius, *plus* well-known websites. An accountant might point to all other local accountants in town *as well as* popular accounting software programs. List these categories of competition, along with the strengths and weaknesses of each, on the worksheet opposite.

Don't forget to include online competition. Even if you're a neighborhood hardware store and are primarily fixated on the Big Box discounter in the next town, don't forget that online ecommerce sites and even eBay are competing for many of the same dollars that you are.

Types of Competition

You face two types of competition: direct and indirect.

Direct Competition: Companies offering products or services much like yours that customers perceive as acceptable alternatives (for example, Honda vs. Toyota or Burger King vs. McDonald's).

Indirect Competition: Companies offering products or services different from yours that meet the same or similar need. Customers can substitute your competitors' offerings for yours (for example, TV advertising vs. radio advertising, train travel vs. air travel, or a children's museum vs. Chuck E. Cheese's).

When developing this section, always consider less obvious sources of competition that attract your customers' attention and dollars.

SAMPLE PLAN:

Types of Competition

Competing with ComputerEase to supply software training services to the target market (businesses making substantial use of computers and having more than 50 employees) are these categories of software training providers:

- Online training/distance learning programs
- Individual independent training consultants
- Local software training companies
- National training companies
- Software developers
- Community college classes
- Trainers from within the targeted companies themselves

Describes the range of competitors

ComputerEase hopes to build its business of developing custom training for corporations that have developed their own software applications for in-house use, as this represents a very high-margin business. Community college classes are generally not suitable for the corporate market, since classes are held in the evenings for at least 10 weeks—conditions that do not meet business customers' needs.

Narrows the competitive field

List the types of businesses, not the specific companies, that compete with you. What are their strengths? What are their weaknesses?

Competition Type	Strengths	Weaknesses

QUICK**TIP**

Shop Your Competition

To collect valuable data and insights for your plan, spend time patronizing your competition. What attracts customers to them? How were you treated? Were their products reasonably priced? Visit your competitors' websites. What features or attributes do they highlight? Get to know your competition through their customers' eyes.

■ Identify your specific competitors

Zero in on specific businesses that compete for your customers on a day-to-day basis (such as the boutique down the street or another neighborhood accountant). Evaluate them in the same way you did your categories of competitors, based on how customers view them and how they operate.

Also note other attributes that may affect their ability to compete, such as:

● Do they have a well-known brand?

● Have they historically been the market leaders?

● Have they been growing?

● Are their marketing efforts focused specifically on your geographic target area?

● Do they have any strategic partnerships with other companies that give them marketing or operational advantages?

● Do they have any exclusive sales or distribution relationships?

Honestly evaluate your competitors. Resist the temptation to dismiss their products or services as inferior to yours. After all, there's a reason they're still in business.

GO GLOBAL: The Competition

Your competition may not just come from across town or even across your country, it may now come from around the world. These international competitors can often sell at prices below yours, even when shipping and fulfillment are added to the final price. This can be a difficult challenge, and you must be aware of this global competition so that you can find ways to distinguish yourself from them and compete successfully. Additionally, not only are products sold internationally, but services are as well. It is typical for many service providers to find themselves competing online with sources from other countries with far lower labor costs. Once again, your challenge is to find ways to make your competitive advantages clear so your value to your customers is apparent even when your price may be substantially higher.

Specific Competitors

Growing and future competition

Online Competitors

The number of online computer software training firms has exploded in recent years. A Google search of "online software training" returned more than 800 million results. Online training has opened markets—including our local market—to both international and local competition. Presently, there are two international companies—one based in the U.K. and one based in Australia—that are potential future competitors. Three national software training companies all have fairly robust online training programs.

Eight local businesses and four individuals in the Vespucci area actively market their software training services. An unknown number of additional individual consultants provide such training on a less visible level. The individual independent consultants generally provide training for just one or two software programs.

Available, but insignificant, training resources

Only one local company has developed a substantial presence with the target market: JMT Training. JMT has operated for more than six years and is the largest local software training company.

Other Competition

The three major national software training companies periodically conduct classes in the Vespucci area. Lesser-known national companies also occasionally provide such services, generally targeting recent purchasers of particular software.

In-house training taught by employees of the targeted companies varies widely in content, form, and quality. Very few companies have "trainers"; most training is provided on an ad hoc basis from supervisors and fellow workers. A conservative interpretation of ComputerEase survey results indicate that at least 20% of such training would be contracted out if satisfactory training could be obtained.

What specific businesses (local, national, worldwide, and online) do you consider to be your direct competition? List them here by name, along with their strengths, weaknesses, and other notable attributes.

Competitor	Strengths	Weaknesses	Other Attributes

QUICK**TIP**

No Market Leader? Lucky for You!

It's difficult to unseat companies that already control a significant share of a market. Want to introduce a new cola-flavored soft drink? It's not easy getting customers away from Coke or Pepsi. You'd have better luck launching an energy drink. Entering a field where market share is widely divided—without clear leaders—gives you a better chance of getting a piece of an emerging market.

■ Determine your competitors' market share

Some competitors are more important than others. In particular, companies commanding the largest share of customers' dollars—in other words, "market share"—present the fiercest competition. Even though these companies may not necessarily provide the best products or most attentive customer service, they're going to be hard to beat. If you're opening a neighborhood hardware store, you're going to have to watch what's going on at Home Depot and Lowe's.

In this section, determine which companies command the largest portion of your market. These competitors are significant because they:

- Tend to define the standard features of a product or service
- Significantly influence customer perceptions of the product or service
- Usually have and spend the resources required to maintain their market share
- Can undercut prices to maintain market share

On the worksheet opposite, list your major competitors along with the percentage of the market each one commands (in revenues and/or units sold). Indicate whether their market share is increasing or decreasing. If yours is an existing business, indicate your market share.

Where to Find Market-Share Data

Trade associations, corporate annual reports, business publications, and independent research firms provide helpful sources of general data to use for your market share section. If you have a library card and an Internet connection, you can access online many of the business databases to which public libraries maintain subscriptions. Many university libraries also have business databases.

SAMPLE PLAN:

Market Share Distribution

The responses to a ComputerEase survey indicate that target companies currently conducting software training utilize providers as follows:

Current Total Market-Share Distribution for Business Software Training in Vespucci, Indiana

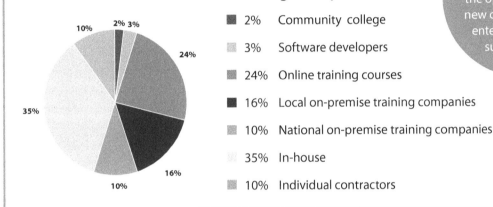

- 2%   Community college
- 3%   Software developers
- 24%   Online training courses
- 16%   Local on-premise training companies
- 10%   National on-premise training companies
- 35%   In-house
- 10%   Individual contractors

> The lack of a dominant market leader offers the opportunity for new competitors to enter the market successfully

---

List your major competitors (general, specific, or both). Who controls what share (portion or percentage) of the market? Are these shares increasing or decreasing? Include yourself, if you currently control part of the market. Use actual data, if available. Otherwise, estimate market-share percentage.

YOUR BUSINESS:	Market Share	Increasing or Decreasing?

COMPETITORS:	Market Share	Increasing or Decreasing?

■ Determine competitive positions

In previous worksheets, you've identified your competitors' strengths, weaknesses, and market share. Now it's time to analyze and rank your competition based on those factors. This shows that you understand the relative strength of your competition and helps you focus on the factors necessary to compete effectively.

On the worksheet below, rank the specific competitors you identified on page 51 from strongest to weakest and provide reasons for their market standing.

Rank your major competitors by name from strongest to weakest. Give the reason for each ranking.

Rank	Competitor	Reason for Ranking

SAMPLE PLAN:

Competitive Analysis

Ranks competition from strongest to weakest

This is how ComputerEase ranks the strengths of its competitors:

1. In-house trainers
2. Online training courses
3. JMT Training
4. National training companies
5. Other local companies
6. Independent contractors

Relative strengths and weaknesses highlighted

By far, the biggest competitor for the dollars spent on business software training is the in-house training department. After that, other online competitors are the biggest hurdle to winning business, as there are other, cheaper alternatives to the ComputerEase products on the market. However, ComputerEase is garnering a growing reputation for delivering high-quality and highly effective training in this crowded field.

JMT is considered the strongest competitor due to its current client base, the personality and sales skills of its owner, Janice Tuffrey, and its potential to associate with national franchise training operations. However, JMT's current training staff and materials are of inconsistent quality, and current clients have expressed dissatisfaction with the lack of quality control. Moreover, JMT lacks skilled management of its financial affairs, resulting in insufficient capital for marketing and updating equipment. No other local companies have either the financial or the personnel resources to adequately respond to a well-organized, sufficiently funded competitor.

National training companies market their services through direct mail or telemarketers and have no local sales force. Their customer base is neither loyal nor particularly satisfied with the service.

The quality of in-house trainers varies widely. However, since these trainers are already on staff, there is little or no additional cost to the customer for using them.

Independent contractors lack a substantial client base and adequate resources to respond to new competition.

■ Highlight your competitive edge

Every business needs some advantages over the competition to attract customers and stay in business. In this section, present yours.

Some typical types of competitive advantages are:

- Price

- Product features

- Convenience (closer to—or faster for—customers)

- Aggressive, effective marketing program

- Choice of industries/types of customers served

- Well-known brand

- Exclusive relationships (distribution, suppliers)

- Operational efficiencies

It's also useful to show how your competitors' weaknesses become your company's strengths. Let's say the market leader in your industry is large and bureaucratic. If your company is small and nimble, explain how you can better respond to sudden changes in market demand. Does your competitor rely on old technology? Highlight your use of state-of-the-art tools that better serve your customers.

SAMPLE PLAN:

Advantages Over Competition

ComputerEase's advantages over its competitors include:

- Its status as an "Authorized Training Center" for major software publishers gives it credibility through joint programs, and the availability of pre-release and steeply discounted software
- Its management team is business-oriented rather than computer-oriented, and is completely focused on the needs of corporate trainers
- Its course developers are certified in the software for which they develop courseware
- It has a proven instructional design methodology for creating, testing, and supporting high-quality courseware
- It is a local, rather than national, provider of on-premise training
- It has a sterling reputation for delivering high-quality service
- It offers ongoing technical support for corporate clients at low cost

Why will your customers choose you over your competition? List your competitive advantages.

■ Evaluate barriers to entry and potential future competition

An important factor to consider is what obstacles, if any, prevent new competition from entering the market. You may be able to take on all your current competitors, but if you're successful, will a flock of new competitors suddenly appear?

As you consider potential future competitors, think about the obstacles they might need to overcome to enter your market. Common obstacles, called "barriers to entry," include:

- Patents and trademarks

- High startup costs

- Substantial, hard-to-find technical or industry expertise

- Market saturation

- Restrictive licensing requirements or regulations

Make a few well-founded predictions about the sources of your competition over the next five years or so. Consider:

- **New companies entering the market.** Good resources for predictions in this area include articles in industry publications or local media.

- **Existing companies expanding their product lines.** Look at companies in related fields and examine their websites for press releases about new product offerings. Once again, check industry media.

Barriers to Entry and Future Competition

It is not easy for new competitors to enter the on-premises training market, which requires a substantial overhead due to rent/leasing expenses, equipment, trainers, and printed materials. Moreover, software providers are becoming increasingly selective about which companies they will allow to serve as "Authorized Training Companies." These relationships are crucial in terms of receiving pre-release, below-cost copies of software to prepare new courses, and for co-sponsoring product introduction events, as well as customer perception.

Highlighted as a ComputerEase advantage earlier

The barriers to entry of online training are much lower, however. All it takes is a single individual designing interactive, online courseware using one of the many authoring programs that exist. Even if the content developer is not technically inclined, he or she can easily find someone to do the coding that makes the content accessible via a standard browser. There are no printing costs, as all the documentation and course materials exist online for the student to download. Of course, there are marketing expenses—to address the challenge of getting noticed in such a crowded field—as well as credibility issues, but simply getting a product to market is relatively cheap and easy to do. Although online competitors can come from anywhere, they will need to understand domestic markets.

Online companies present a major threat

List your potential future competitors.

_____

_____

_____

_____

_____

_____

_____

What obstacles might new competition face in trying to enter your market? What are the barriers to entry?

_____

_____

_____

_____

_____

■ Pulling it all together: The Competition

To be an effective competitor, you have to understand what you're up against. Honestly evaluating your competition, their strengths as well as their weaknesses, arms you to survive. If you think you have *no* competition, think again. If you're filling a genuine market need, then there certainly are—or will be—other companies that want a piece of the action.

Synthesize the information you've gathered into a concise, convincing description of your competition, one that highlights your competitive advantages.

What types of businesses compete with you? (See worksheet on page 49.)
_____
_____

Who are your specific competitors? (See worksheet on page 51.)
_____
_____
_____

What share (portion) of the market does each competitor control?
(See worksheet on page 53.)
_____
_____
_____

How would you rank your competitors (in terms of market position)?
(See worksheet on page 54.)
_____
_____
_____

What are your competitive advantages? (See worksheet on page 57.)
_____
_____
_____

Who will your future competitors be, and what barriers to entry do they face?
(See worksheet on page 59.)
_____
_____
_____

5

Accomplishments

In this step you'll:

☐ Summarize your marketing message

☐ Describe your offline marketing vehicles

☐ Describe your online and social media marketing vehicles

☐ Identify additional offline marketing and sales strategies

☐ Describe your sales team

☐ Pulling it all together: Marketing and Sales Plan

Time-Saving Tools

You'll complete this section more quickly if you have any of the following handy:

☐ Marketing collateral (brochures, advertisements, press releases)

☐ Marketing budget and/or expenses

☐ Information about your sales team

☐ Sales history (for an existing business)

☐ Sales forecasts

☐ Positive reviews you've received on review sites; number of social media followers on various platforms

You know you have a good product or service, but can you convince customers to buy it? This is where your marketing and sales strategy comes in. It describes your plans for spreading the word about your product or service and selling to your customers.

Because your marketing and sales plan outlines your strategy for securing customers and sales, it's a critical key to your success. Investors and lenders want to see:

- A realistic, cost-effective marketing approach to informing potential customers about your products or services and the benefits offered

- An effective sales force

- Appropriate sales techniques and methods

KEY TO SUCCESS

Doing Well by Doing Good

In a highly competitive market, you can distinguish your company—and increase customer loyalty—by practicing socially and environmentally responsible policies: ensuring fair treatment of employees, providing decent pay, using ethical business practices, and minimizing waste and pollution. Not only will you do the right thing for your community and your environment, you'll increase profits as customers will respect and feel good about patronizing your company. For more on social responsibility, see pages 90-91.

Marketing vs. Sales

Marketing and sales, while closely related, have very different functions.

Marketing activities make customers aware of your product or service and the benefits it offers. Marketing activities include advertising (print, radio, TV, online), producing collateral material (brochures, product information sheets), developing company websites, doing public relations (press releases, events), attending trade show exhibitions, and offering free sample giveaways.

Sales activities are direct interactions with your potential customers to solicit and procure orders or to make an immediate sale. Sales activities include in-person sales at a customer's home or place of business, telemarketing, ecommerce, direct mail, online sales, or selling merchandise in person at a store, trade show, or other event.

■ Summarize your marketing message

Every business sends a message in its marketing. To be most effective, base this message on the strategic position your company stakes out in the marketplace—the way you intend to distinguish yourself from your competitors. For instance, if you are competing on price, your message is "low-price leader." If you're competing on convenience, your message might be "one-hour service." Perhaps you are exploiting a particular niche in the market, such as "attorneys specializing in estate planning" or "software for architects."

Such messages set you apart from the competition and help customers quickly decide if you present an appropriate option for their needs and buying priorities.

Words to Sell By

Some of the best company slogans focus on their customers' needs and desires rather than their product's attributes. Here are a few examples. Be cautious, however, when attempting this approach yourself; it takes an enormous marketing budget to make these indirect taglines memorable.

SLOGAN	COMPANY	MOTIVATION
Just Do It	Nike	Customers want to reach their fitness goals
Because You're Worth It	L'Oréal	Bolsters the customer's self-image
You're in Good Hands with Allstate	Allstate	Customers seek security and protection
There's an App for That	Apple	Customers can do whatever they want on the iPhone
Red Bull Gives You Wings	Red Bull	Customers want an energy boost

SAMPLE PLAN:

Marketing Message

ComputerEase's slogan, "We speak your language," is designed to reassure its primary market: large corporate customers. The slogan implies both that the software training itself will be comprehensible and that ComputerEase understands the needs of the business customer.

As a play on the word "computerese," the name is designed to be memorable, with the added implication that the company makes dealing with computers easy.

ComputerEase prominently features its slogan, "We speak your language," on all its marketing materials, on its company website, and at the bottom of email messages.

Marketing message and slogan

How do you position your company in the market? How do you want customers to think of your company? Summarize your message in 50 words or fewer.

Do you have a company tagline or slogan? Include it here.

QUICK**TIP**

A Good Fit?

Make sure your marketing approach and the marketing vehicles you choose are a good fit for the type and size of business you run. A small graphic design firm may be most successful spending its marketing dollars by joining and attending local entrepreneur network groups, while a retail store may do better advertising in a local newspaper.

■ Describe your offline marketing vehicles

Once you have summarized what you want to tell potential customers, explain your plan for getting your company's name and marketing message out. Will you advertise? If so, where and how often? Exhibit at trade shows? If so, at which shows and how much will that cost? You'll likely use a combination of offline and online marketing vehicles. Online and social media marketing vehicles are covered next.

Since every marketing vehicle costs money, carefully plan how you'll spend your marketing dollars. Some options:

- Product brochures
- Print media advertisements
- Broadcast media ads (radio, network and cable TV)
- Joining networking groups
- Public relations activities
- Direct mail
- Word-of-mouth marketing
- Customer loyalty programs

On the worksheet opposite, list the types of marketing vehicles you'll use. Also, indicate how often you plan to use them and how much it will cost. You'll use these figures later, in Step 9, when you prepare your financials.

A Magazine for Fenceposts?

While the mainstream press exposes your ad to more people, highly targeted publications reach those more likely to buy. If you sell specialized fences, you'll reach more potential customers advertising in a trade journal, like *FencePost* magazine or *World Fence News*, than in a general newspaper. There are trade publications for just about every industry or interest; locate them by searching online or check the listing of trade associations at PlanningShop's website: **www.PlanningShop.com/associations**.

Offline Marketing Vehicles

ComputerEase uses a combination of offline, online, and social media marketing techniques. One of the most successful marketing campaigns has been the company's ongoing direct mail program. A schedule of ComputerEase's downtown classes is sent out every two months to the target audience of 4,500 recipients. For leads, ComputerEase purchases lists of human resource directors and another list of local subscribers to a leading computer magazine. All prior students are also included in the direct mail program.

The firm also sponsors ads in *Corporate Trainer Magazine*, and is one of the sponsors of the largest software training conference in North America.

For its on-premise marketing, ComputerEase focuses on face-to-face solicitation of human resource and training directors of large local corporations.

What offline marketing vehicles will you use to deliver your message? (Advertising? Direct mail? Trade shows? Networking events? Public relations?)

How frequently do you intend to use these marketing vehicles?

How much do you expect to spend on these marketing activities each month?

QUICK**TIP**

Use Social Media Sites to:

- Spread the word and create buzz about your products or services

- Design campaigns to target your specific audience

- Create your own group to get feedback from customers

- Build referral sources and networking connections

- Engage with prospects and customers

- Enhance your credibility by contributing meaningful content to others' sites

- Announce sales and special offers

■ Outline your online and social media marketing vehicles

Like anything else in your business, your online and social media marketing requires a strategy to execute successfully. Social media marketing, for example, offers an enormous range of opportunities, with new ones being developed constantly as new technologies emerge and entrepreneurs devise innovative ways to communicate. But without a plan, social media marketing can take up a colossal amount of time, with little benefit. In this section, you'll create a thoughtful, effective plan for all of your online and social media marketing.

Some options include:

- Company website
- Social media sites such as Facebook, Instagram, Twitter, LinkedIn, Pinterest
- SEO, SEM, and online ads
- Email newsletters and blogs
- Daily deals
- Review sites
- Mobile marketing

As with the previous worksheet, in Step 9 you'll use the figures you come up with on the worksheet opposite, when you prepare your financials.

Email Newsletters

While both social media and email newsletters can be extremely effective to get the word out about your business, there is a big difference between the two marketing vehicles. With social media, you don't own the list of your followers' email addresses—Facebook, Instagram, or Twitter do. If you're locked out of your social media accounts suddenly, you'll have no way of reaching those prospects you worked so hard to acquire. So at the start of your business, be sure to capture the email addresses of your potential customers to build your list. Then start sending out email newsletters regularly. You'll build your business, stay in front of your customers and prospects—and you own your list of contacts.

SAMPLE PLAN:

Online and Social Media Marketing Vehicles

Most of ComputerEase's marketing for its online products is done—appropriately enough—online and through social media. In order to network with businesses seeking computer training, ComputerEase maintains a profile on LinkedIn. It also has an active Facebook page and Twitter feed, both of which it uses to engage students, provide customer support, post updates and schedules of classes, and create online buzz about the company. The company also has a YouTube channel, where it has posted—and it updates—a series of helpful, short, simple "how-to" videos that address common problems people encounter when using certain popular software programs. Entry-level employees, typically recent business graduates from one of Vespucci's seven universities or colleges, execute the social media campaigns, making the programs very cost effective.

ComputerEase recognizes that more and more of its clients conduct business using their smartphones and tablets. The company maintains a mobile version of its website, and is listed on local business sites such as Yelp, Google My Business, and Bing Places for Business. The firm buys keywords from the major search engines so that its ads show up anytime a user performs a search using those words.

Additionally, ComputerEase also sends out every month, to a growing list of corporate trainers, a highly regarded email newsletter that explores best practices in technology training.

What online and social media marketing vehicles will you use to deliver your message?
(Facebook, Instagram, and Twitter? Online ads? Email newsletters?)

_____

_____

_____

Which staff will manage your social media activities? How much time will they spend weekly?

_____

_____

_____

How much do you expect to spend on online marketing each month? What is your annual marketing budget for *all* marketing activities?

_____

_____

_____

Website Essentials

Every business must have a website. It may be robust—where you sell products directly to customers, or answer customer service inquiries—or it may be quite simple. Even if you never sell anything directly online, you still need a website. As the public face of your company, your website provides customers, prospects, and investors with a way to interact with and learn about your company's products and services, background, clients or customers, team, and more. And it helps determine whether they'll trust you enough to take the next step and actually do business with you.

Getting a website up and running can be either an easy task, involving just a little time and money, or an enormous undertaking, requiring months of work and many thousands of dollars. It all depends on how big and complicated a site you want, how much interactivity you want and need, whether your site must be able to support ecommerce capabilities, and, more important, whether you create a custom site or instead use templates and services that devise turnkey solutions.

Turnkey solutions for websites often include everything from domain registration to hosting, design templates, a menu of website services (such as "shopping carts"), standard forms, and so on. These make launching a website relatively easy and inexpensive. Whichever route you take, identify who on your team will be involved, including any IT help you'll need.

Use the worksheet on the following page to determine your site's content.

Make It Mobile

Mobile devices have transformed the way customers deal with local businesses. How long has it been since you used your smartphone to find a business? To reserve a table at a restaurant? To get directions? Likely, not long. You don't have to develop a gee-whiz app or use every mobile method available in order to reach the increasing number of people searching for businesses like yours on their mobile devices. You do, however, at least need a mobile version of your website.

Types of Websites

Websites can be categorized generally along the following lines:

- Brochure sites
- Ecommerce sites
- Content sites
- Lead generation sites
- Portal sites
- Customer service sites

When deciding how you'll use your website, keep in mind the cost of ongoing maintenance. If your site will require frequent updates and changes, make sure it is designed in such a way that you can easily make those changes.

Check off and describe the elements you plan to include on your website:

☐ Home page:

☐ Overview of products/services:

☐ About your company:

☐ Contact info:

☐ Social media accounts:

☐ Privacy policy:

☐ Relevant content:

☐ Media/Press section:

☐ Testimonials/Awards/Client lists:

☐ Newsletter sign-up:

☐ Samples/Demos:

☐ Catalog:

☐ User-generated content:

☐ Customer service info and/or forms:

☐ FAQs (Frequently Asked Questions):

☐ Site map/Search box:

☐ Investor information:

☐ Enhanced visuals or sound:

☐ Other:

QUICK**TIP**

Split the Cost

If you're selling another company's products or services —or if they're selling yours— ask them to participate in co-op advertising or promotions. Since it's in both of your interests to make sales, they'll often agree to split, or share, marketing expenses. For instance, if you run a sporting goods store, a ski manufacturer may split the cost of an ad in your local newspaper promoting a sale of their product at your store.

■ Identify any additional marketing and sales strategies

In addition to traditional advertising and marketing vehicles, many businesses work with other companies to promote their businesses and make sales. Some of these strategies include:

- **Strategic Partnerships.** Associating with another company to jointly promote each other's products or services or to have them promote your company as part of their offerings.

- **Licensing Agreements.** Licensing the rights to your product or service to another company, usually enabling them to sell your product or service under their name.

- **Distribution Agreements.** Arranging with another company to market and sell your product or service for you. Distributors often have their own sales force as well as warehouse and shipping facilities.

- **Using Wholesalers.** Wholesalers buy in bulk, then divide the goods into smaller quantities to sell to many retailers.

- **Working with Agents/Brokers.** These are individuals who sell your products or services, usually on a commission basis.

GO GLOBAL:
Marketing Internationally

In today's connected world, it's easier than ever to find and serve customers worldwide. While your domestic market may seem like a large enough target market to pursue, you should also at least consider expanding your potential customer base internationally. Even if you don't directly target global customers, it's likely that you'll have customers throughout the world, especially if you have an online presence. And remember, international customers may find you even if you do not actively seek them.

SAMPLE PLAN:

Marketing and Sales Strategies

Marketing partnerships

ComputerEase partners with leading software publishers on many collaborative marketing activities. These include sharing the cost of cooperative advertisements placed in regional computer publications, sponsoring special events to introduce corporate clients to the publishers' new software, and sponsoring a trade show booth at the regional human resource directors' annual convention.

As one of the key sponsors of the corporate training world's largest conference on software training, ComputerEase has earned a lot of credibility through its presentations and executive speeches by Vice President of Marketing Ishaan Permaul and President Charlotte Alexander. Additionally, ComputerEase has agreements with three of the top national software distributors and the largest hardware reseller chain as well as a growing network of computer consultants to "bundle" its training courses with new hardware and software sales for a discounted fee.

Strategic partnerships

What other marketing and sales strategies do you use, if any? (Include tactics such as co-op advertising, third-party distribution or licensing agreements, and other strategic partnerships.)

■ Describe your sales team

Your sales team provides your most important link to your customers— and to your profits. These staff members not only sell your product or service, they also have access to critical information about your customers' needs, desires, and buying habits.

The structure of your sales force reflects your sales methods: if you rely on face-to-face sales calls, you are likely to have salespeople on staff or use independent sales representatives. If you rely on telemarketing, you may employ part-time personnel or contract with an outsource telemarketing company.

On the worksheet opposite, discuss the structure of your sales force. Detail whether you use:

- Full-time personnel
- Part-time personnel
- Independent sales representatives
- Employees of a different company

If you have determined that demand exists in other parts of the world for your products or services, you also need to evaluate how you will make and fulfill those sales. Explain how you pay your salespeople. Do they get straight salary? Straight commission? Base salary and commission? What percentage commission? Describe bonuses and other incentives you provide.

Types of Sales Reps

The responsibilities of sales teams generally fall into one of three categories:

Inside Sales. They make sales while on the company premises. Telemarketers and retail store sales staff are inside salespeople.

Outside Sales. They visit customers to solicit orders and often nurture ongoing professional relationships with them. Pharmaceutical company agents who visit doctors and hospitals and employees who sell products in person to key clients are all examples of outside salespeople.

Independent Sales Representatives. These independent contractors (nonemployees) sell your products to a territory or to a range of customers. They may represent only your business; however, they often also represent products from a number of related companies at once.

Sales Team

Since ComputerEase's primary target market is mid- to large-size companies, it has to carefully tailor its sales pitch to the buyers of corporate training—either in-house training managers or human resource professionals. It does this through a small telesales team of three contractors who are each paid $20 per hour plus commissions. Their primary job: to get past the primary "gatekeeper" and then pass the lead onto Vice President of Marketing Ishaan Permaul or President and CEO Charlotte Alexander.

All queries coming in through the website are first screened by the receptionist, who doubles as the customer service representative, and who responds to each one immediately and personally, and passes the lead onto Permaul or Alexander. Each website inquiry is called back within 24 hours. A part-time channel administrator is in charge of handling all requests for information or orders that come in through software or hardware resellers or consultants.

Additionally, all company personnel are considered members of the sales team. Even the software trainers themselves participate in monthly sales training meetings, and all employees receive financial bonuses if the company reaches overall sales goals.

> Additional motivation to make sales

Who makes sales in your company? Do you have designated salespeople? If so, how many?

How are their jobs structured? (Inside sales? Outside sales? Independent contractors?)

What are the highlights of your sales team's experience? How many combined years? Do any have a successful track record with products/services similar to yours?

How do you pay them? (Commission? Commission plus base? Salary? Bonuses? Incentives?)

How do you train them? What do you do to continually motivate them?

■ Pulling it all together: Marketing and Sales Plan

To stay in business, you have to reach customers and secure sales. That is why this section of your plan is particularly important and likely to be reviewed closely by prospective investors or lenders. In this section, potential funders want to see that your marketing and sales methods are appropriate for your business, and that your sales force is both large enough and well-enough trained to secure the sales levels necessary to sustain your business.

Synthesize all the marketing and sales information you've gathered into a clear, concise description of your marketing and sales plan.

What is your marketing message? (See worksheet on page 65.)

_____

_____

_____

_____

Which marketing vehicles will you use? (See worksheets on pages 67 and 69.)

_____

_____

_____

_____

What other marketing and sales strategies will you employ? (See worksheet on page 73.)

_____

_____

_____

Who is on your sales team, and how is it structured? (See worksheet on page 75.)

_____

_____

_____

_____

6

Accomplishments

In this step you'll:

☐ Describe key operational factors

☐ Outline your technology plan

☐ Highlight your corporate advantage

☐ Find solutions to potential problems

☐ Describe your commitment to social responsibility and sustainability

☐ Pulling it all together: Operations

Time-Saving Tools

You'll complete this section more quickly if you have any of the following handy:

☐ Maps of facilities

☐ Addresses of facilities

☐ Technological diagrams

☐ Work and production flow charts

☐ Operations-related financial records

Step 6

Operations

How are you actually going to run your business? The Operations section of your business plan briefly describes how you execute the basic functions of your company: manufacturing or creating your product or service, keeping on top of inventory, and delivering your product or service to your customer.

Emphasize any operational aspects that give your company a competitive edge. If you've found a way to cut costs and increase profit margins, by using innovative production methods or less-expensive suppliers, highlight those aspects in your business plan.

Operational aspects of your business plan include:

- Location and facilities

- Production and quality control

- Inventory management

- Supply and distribution

- Order fulfillment and customer service

- Equipment and technology

- Financial control systems

- Social responsibility and sustainability

How much detail you'll offer on each of these aspects depends on your type of business. For example, a catering company would focus on facilities and cost control; a limousine service would focus on equipment (vehicles) and perhaps technology (for dispatching). For more information on each of these components, see *Elements of an Operations Plan* on pages 80-81.

KEY TO SUCCESS

Your goal in this section is to show:

- You've thought through what it takes to make your company function.

- You are capable of managing those functions on a day-to-day basis.

- The reasons for any changes—and additional costs—in operations for an existing business (particularly if you're seeking funding).

Elements of an Operations Plan

- **Location and facilities.** The place you set up shop affects your ability to do business. Why did you choose this location or building? Proximity to your target market? Low rent or attractive lease terms? Easy access to transportation?

  How are the facilities arranged to make doing business easier? Describe the benefits of your location and facilities, *or*, if you're seeking funding to move to a new location, focus on the benefits of moving to a more appropriate place.

- **Production and quality control.** Every business has a production process. If you make a product, your process is the way you fabricate raw materials to create a new item; if yours is a service business, you'll have a method for designing and delivering your service to customers. Focus on issues such as your production methods, capacity, cost-saving procedures, and the methods you use to ensure consistent quality and reduce both waste and environmental impact.

- **Inventory management.** If you make or sell a product, how you manage inventory levels has a direct impact on your bottom line. You can have too much money invested in inventory that just sits around, or, conversely, not enough inventory to fill orders. Briefly describe the ways in which you manage your inventory levels to produce the highest profits.

- **Supply and distribution.** Whom do you rely on to provide you with the goods coming into your company, and whom do you rely on to help sell the goods going out? Describe the relationships you have with key suppliers or distributors and wholesalers. Are your supply channels and distribution methods reliable? Do you have long-standing relationships or favorable credit terms with suppliers and distributors? Highlight the relationships that give your company added stability.

- **Order fulfillment and customer service.** Once you have produced your product or planned for your service, how do you get it to your customer? What are your packaging, shipping, and warehousing systems? Do you have procedures for handling customer complaints or soliciting customer feedback? Show that you have an efficient system for fulfilling customers' orders and responding to their concerns.

- **Equipment and technology.** Perhaps you are using state-of-the-art or advanced equipment and technology to run your business or produce your product. If so, discuss ways in which this improves operational efficiency, saves money, and gives you a competitive edge.

- **Financial control systems.** Do you have procedures in place to make certain that financial matters are handled promptly and accurately? How are invoices sent out? How are your bills paid? Do you have a system to ensure that key managers are regularly reviewing financial information? A system for fraud prevention?

- **Social responsibility and sustainability.** Do you have methods to reduce waste and excess energy use? Do you use recycled materials in production? Do your suppliers use sustainable business practices? It often pays to highlight those practices that show you have thought about the impact of your actions on your community and your environment.

Keep It Simple

Rather than an operations manual, the Operations section of your business plan is a brief overview demonstrating that you understand the nitty-gritty details that make your business work.

If your operations are very simple (a home-based graphic design firm, for instance), you can omit this section altogether. However, you should then include a paragraph or two in your Company Description outlining your basic operations, such as what technology you use.

On the other hand, if your business is new, expanding, or complicated, go into more detail in your Operations section. Just remember: it's not necessary—or advisable—to provide a step-by-step guide to how your company works. Save that for an operations manual you use internally.

QUICK**TIP**

Other Operational Issues

In addition to the operational elements listed in detail on the previous pages, depending on the size and nature of your business, a variety of other operational concerns will face your company. These include:

- Protecting the safety of your workers

- Insurance and legal issues

- Dealing with government regulations

- Research and development

- Contingency planning

- Exporting goods

■ Determine key operations elements

In this area, highlight the most important operational aspects of your business. Review the various operational aspects described in *Elements of an Operations Plan* on pages 80-81. Focus on those most central to your company's success. You don't have to include each element in your business plan, just the ones at your company's core. A catering company, for instance, could highlight its convenient and well-equipped commercial kitchen facilities, critical for enabling the company to handle large orders.

If yours is an unusual business—or if you are seeking funding from a source not familiar with your industry—explain enough of the basic operations to enable your readers to understand how a company like yours functions.

GO GLOBAL:

Operational Issues

Virtually any aspect of your operations can have a global component today, regardless of the size of your business. With apps like Zoom, Skype, WhatsApp, and other technologies, it's both easy and inexpensive to do business internationally, even to have staff members, critical subcontractors, or vendors and suppliers located halfway around the world. As you begin to consider your international operations, it is useful to understand two widely used terms:

- **Outsourcing:** Using an outside company or vendor to perform some functions of your business.

- **Offshoring:** Having some of a company's operations performed in another country, either by using foreign vendors or by transferring operations to that country.

SAMPLE PLAN:

Key Elements of Operations

Describes a key operational factor

A key element of ComputerEase's operations is its Corporate Training Center, located at 987 South Main Street in Vespucci. The Center currently consists of 20 student computer stations, equipped with all the major business software programs, an instructor's computer station and projection equipment, and state-of-the-art technology enabling the instructor to monitor exactly what each student does.

The Corporate Training Center is vital because most of ComputerEase's corporate customers have limited, if any, extra computer facilities on their premises appropriate for conducting on-site corporate classes. Thus, ComputerEase can only grow to an adequate level of income by having well-equipped training facilities of its own to offer.

Explains reason for key factor's importance

For its online training courses, ComputerEase decided not to buy and manage its own servers or to build its own data center, but rather to outsource that to a managed hosting vendor that provides a turnkey solution for all hardware/software needs and maintenance, backups, upgrades.

List the operational factors most critical to your business and how you deal with them, then explain why they are important. You do not need to discuss every one of these factors here, only those key to your operations.

Your approach to:	Reason for importance:
Location/Facilities:	
Production/Quality Control:	
Inventory Control:	
Supply/Distribution:	
Order Fulfillment/Customer Service:	
Equipment/Technology:	
Financial Control Systems:	
Environmental Impact:	
Other:	

■ Outline your technology plan

Technology is central to running any business. This section helps you outline your technology needs.

Some companies are specifically in the business of developing or exploiting new technology. In these companies, potential investors want detailed information about the nature of the technology. This description can be a separate section of the plan, describing the basic concept and features of the technology with a level of detail geared to the expertise of the potential reader.

In any business, you'll need both hardware —physical devices such as laptops, tablets, mobile phones, printers, perhaps servers— and software applications. Start slowly but do your homework.

Consider:

- **Cost.** Both your initial cost of acquisition and ongoing costs, as well as maintenance for physical devices and on-premise applications.

- **Security.** How safe are both your data and your devices? Often data stored in the cloud is more secure than data stored only on laptops. Also, can you easily block access for employees once they leave your employ?

- **Mobility.** You want to be able to access your data from virtually anywhere. On-premise software may limit your mobility.

- **Scalability.** Can you easily increase or decrease the number of users as your business grows or changes, "turning on" or "turning off" resources as needed?

GO GLOBAL:
Technology Concerns

Although most technology has been developed for international standards, some issues may arise from things such as electrical currents or telecommunications standards. Some mobile phones will not work in other countries, for example. Occasionally some governments may place limits on the use or access of technology. For instance, certain countries limit their citizens' access to particular search engines or social media websites. Other countries put limits on what can be advertised on auction sites. If you are operating your technology across borders, consider any conflicts or problems that are likely to arise.

SAMPLE PLAN:

Technology

The most critical component of our technology plan is making certain our course developers and instructors are fully capable of teaching the newest software and applications. To that end, they receive prerelease copies of software programs and prerelease training from major software manufacturers and application developers.

Key to success is staying on the cutting edge of instructional design technology. We partner with experts in the field to stay abreast of new developments in interactive online courseware and add enhancements as they emerge. We also develop training materials and applications for smartphones, iPads, and other electronic tablets.

ComputerEase offers online courses which enable us to expedite our geographic reach into other parts of the U.S. and also into any English-speaking country.

Our Training Centers are also critical. One Training Center is already in operation, and we anticipate opening a second center by January 2023. This center will have 20–30 of the most up-to-date personal computers, 3–4 printers, overhead projection equipment, and other audiovisual equipment. We lease our computers for the Training Centers rather than purchase them; this enables us to always offer students the latest equipment.

Our company website contains background information on the company and lists the schedule and descriptions of training classes for both online and in-person training sessions. Students of corporate training classes taking place in our center can register on our website and access password-protected areas to receive additional assistance after completing their training sessions.

Demonstrates how a technology-based company stays up to date

Details necessary hardware

Describes website and its capabilities

Using this form as a guide, summarize the key technology concerns and technology needs of your business.

Website:

Software applications:

Hardware:

Telecommunications:

Personnel: (Specify in-house or outsourced)

■ Highlight your operational advantages

Here's where you can make your company—and your business plan—shine. Are you implementing, or devising, any operational efficiencies or innovations that give you an advantage over your competitors or increase profits? If so, be sure to highlight them here.

In this section, demonstrate how the operational choices you've made enhance your company's bottom line and give you an edge over your competition. For example, if a florist found a method of purchasing flowers directly from growers, rather than from wholesalers, she'd indicate how this improves her profit margins.

Explain any trade-offs you've made by choosing a particular procedure, piece of equipment, or technology. The florist, for instance, might need to purchase additional refrigeration units, and will incur additional costs, as a result of buying flowers directly, but could also show how those costs will be recouped in higher profits within a 12-month period.

Which, if any, of your operational procedures or innovations enhance efficiencies, minimize costs, and/or maximize profits?

How do these compare with other companies in your industry?

How do they give you a competitive edge?

What, if any, are the cost/benefit trade-offs of implementing these methods?

Operational Advantages

Outsourcing its data center operations created several key advantages for ComputerEase. First, this strategic operations decision allows ComputerEase to focus on what it does best—design classes to efficiently and effectively teach computer software—rather than worry about the nuts and bolts of the underlying supporting technology. ComputerEase doesn't have to worry about finding and retaining qualified technical staff, or expending large capital investments in hardware and software. Instead, it pays a predictable monthly fee to the outsourcer, which it can write off on its taxes as operating expense. This also gives ComputerEase the flexibility to grow as needed: rather than having to constantly buy more hardware and software as the business grows, it merely contracts for additional capacity from the outsourcing firm.

Having its own training classroom enables ComputerEase to enjoy higher profit margins than its competitors.

While maintaining a classroom incurs the additional costs of rent and equipment, training classes held at ComputerEase's Corporate Training Center produce higher profit margins than classes conducted at customers' facilities ("on-site classes").

In comparison to classes held at ComputerEase's own classroom, on-site classes typically have fewer students per session, incur additional instructor and transportation costs, and increase wear and tear on equipment.

Drawbacks of alternate methods

While ComputerEase charges higher fees per student for on-site classes, the market will not bear prices that truly absorb the increased costs.

Moreover, the potential customer base for Training Center classes is substantially larger than that for on-site programs. More businesses can afford to send employees to scheduled classes at ComputerEase's Corporate Training Center—or have a class developed for them at the Center—than can incur the costs and disruption of an on-site program.

Benefits include lower costs and larger customer base

ComputerEase management chose to lease rather than purchase its Corporate Training Center equipment and negotiated favorable lease terms with Wait's Computer Emporium, enabling the company to upgrade its computers every 12 months. This not only significantly reduced the initial capital outlay, which would have exceeded $100,000, but also ensures that ComputerEase always has the latest technology for its students—a useful marketing, as well as educational, advantage.

With the funds now being sought, the company will open a second Corporate Training Center in the city of Whitten Park, where many of its corporate customers are located.

Additional advantage of state-of-the-art technology

■ Address current—or potential—operational challenges

Most companies continually face changes and challenges in their operations, such as the need to update technology or equipment, find new facilities, or implement new processes or procedures. Perhaps you're developing your business plan to raise funds to deal with these needed changes. If so, you'll need to outline the problems you're currently experiencing, or the ones you anticipate in the near future, along with how you propose to address them.

In this section, describe any operational problems and potential solutions, addressing these questions:

- What operational issues currently reduce your competitiveness or profitability?

- What operational problems do you anticipate encountering in the near future?

- How do these problems affect your ability to do business or attract customers?

- What is your current plan for overcoming these problems?

- What are the costs associated with your solutions?

Innovative Operations

Are you creating a brand-new product? If so, you may face additional operational hurdles. Is there a distribution system in place to get your goods to market? Are there adequate sources or supplies of raw materials? Have you figured out how to manufacture your product profitably?

In your business plan, briefly describe the issues facing you as an innovator and your planned solutions (without giving away trade secrets). Doing so shows that you are smart enough to realize there are added challenges when you're on the cutting edge.

Operational Challenges

A major part of the cost of high-quality corporate training is the documentation and accompanying materials provided to each student. Although ComputerEase leverages all the development, writing, and updating work that goes into these materials for both its online and on-premises courses, that's still the single biggest expense the company incurs. Materials are revised for each new software upgrade, so their average lifespan is less than 12 months.

To reduce materials costs, we develop all of our training materials, such as course manuals, for online publication only. Instead of receiving printed materials, each student receives a password to access training materials. This also helps the company be more green, by reducing paper use and waste. Although ComputerEase pays more in technical support than it would if course materials were printed, the net result is substantially increased profit margins.

A major operational challenge is staying on the cutting edge of instructional techniques, as technology evolves quickly and users demand richer experiences. This includes adopting updated online courseware platforms and incorporating into the training materials more-costly features such as audio and video.

Current problem

Current approach to problem

Shows long-term solution to problem

What operational challenges currently face your company?

_____

_____

_____

How are you dealing with these issues?

_____

_____

_____

What operational challenges do you see in the future?

_____

_____

_____

How much will it cost for you to adequately address these challenges?

_____

_____

QUICK**TIP**

Social Entrepreneurship

Social entrepreneurship differs from social responsibility. All companies today should strive to be responsible. This doesn't mean they all have to make the social good the primary driver of their existence. This is what social entrepreneurs do. They wish to solve critical social problems. But they also want to be profitable. They believe that by using entrepreneurial approaches—including having a profit motive—they can make substantial changes.

■ Describe your commitment to social responsibility

If you are especially committed to social responsibility or are a social entrepreneur, highlight these facts in your operations section. In this section, outline in what ways you will act on that commitment and how your commitment to social responsibility benefits your company. Do your social responsibility activities increase your company visibility? Are you able to recruit high-quality potential employees as a result of your social commitment? What kinds of contacts with other companies does your involvement in the community bring about?

Your company can choose from a number of ways to be involved in social responsibility activities. The first, of course, is to be a good corporate citizen. Others include:

- Treating employees fairly
- Providing decent pay
- Using ethical business practices
- Participating in or initiating programs that benefit the community
- Donating a set percentage of profits or sales
- Minimizing waste and pollution

GO GLOBAL: Social Responsibility

Responsible business people facing global issues such as lax labor laws, pay scales below a living wage, unhealthy working conditions, and child labor, must ask themselves how they will deal with these situations from both a business and a moral perspective. Promoting positive, socially responsible business practices helps make you a force for improving working and environmental conditions worldwide.

SAMPLE PLAN:

Social Responsibility and Sustainability

To implement social responsibility into the company's operations, ComputerEase has partnered with the Downtown Vespucci Community Center to provide free computer training programs for inner-city youth, low-income residents, and "welfare-to-work" program participants. These training programs are held once a month at ComputerEase's downtown Computer Training Center when the Center would otherwise not be in use (Sundays/some evenings, etc.). ComputerEase management and instructors have volunteered their time to conduct these sessions, and the company contributes meals, transportation expenses for volunteer instructors, and a branded T-shirt for all program participants.

ComputerEase's biggest opportunity for improving sustainability comes from curbing our energy consumption. For this reason, we will invest in the installation of solar panels on the roof of our new Training Center, which will generate half of our electricity. In addition, we will lease the most energy-efficient computers and electronics to reduce the number of solar panels necessary to power our new LEED certified building.

> Shows a company-wide commitment to giving back to the community

> Specific details for reducing carbon footprint

List your social responsibility activities or projects.

In what ways will you participate?

What period of time are you willing to commit for? (e.g., days, weeks, year)

In what ways will you commit to sustainability?

■ Pulling it all together: Operations

The Operations section of your business plan should not be overly detailed—save the specifics for your own internal operations manual. By describing the highlights of your operations, you show that you know how to make your company work on a day-to-day basis. This helps you to analyze any problems you're facing and think through solutions. And it increases confidence in your ability to structure and manage an efficient and profitable company.

Draw from the information you provided in the worksheets in this Step to complete this final worksheet and develop the Operations section of your plan.

What are the key components of your operations structure? (See worksheet on page 83.)

_____

_____

Summarize your key technology concerns and technology needs. (See worksheet on page 85.)

_____

_____

In what ways do your operations structure and/or elements give you a competitive advantage? (See worksheet on page 86.)

_____

_____

What are some of your current or potential operational challenges? How do you plan to overcome those challenges? (See worksheet on page 89.)

_____

_____

What are your plans for social responsibility and sustainability? (See worksheet on page 91.)

_____

_____

Accomplishments

In this step you'll:

- ☐ Highlight your key team members
- ☐ Forecast future management needs
- ☐ Describe your staffing structure
- ☐ Identify members of your board of directors and advisory committee as well as any consultants
- ☐ Pulling it all together: Management Structures

Time-Saving Tools

You'll complete this section more quickly if you have any of the following handy:

- ☐ Resumes of key managers
- ☐ Organizational charts
- ☐ Salary and payroll numbers
- ☐ Biographies of board members, advisors, and consultants

Management Structure

Many readers of your business plan will turn to the Management section first. They want to know who's running the shop. Investors and lenders want assurance that the company is managed by competent leaders. In this section, you want to show that:

- The key members of your staff are qualified to run your business.

- You understand what additional staff, if any, is necessary.

- Your staffing levels and roles are appropriate and sufficient to achieve results.

- You've turned to qualified outside advisors when necessary.

 **KEY TO SUCCESS**

Make Your Stars Shine

Do you have any well-known, highly accomplished people associated with your company? Have any of your key personnel had experience at well-regarded companies? If so, highlight these individuals prominently in your Management section and in your Executive Summary. Well-known names increase readers' confidence in your business plan.

How you prepare this section depends on how you're going to use your business plan. If you're developing your plan to raise money, focus primarily on the backgrounds of your management team. Summarize their relevant qualifications in a concise and objective style. If, on the other hand, you are creating a plan for internal use, concentrate instead on your staffing structure and the gaps in your team.

If yours is a very small business, and you are the key—or only—employee, you can omit this section. (However, be sure to emphasize your skills and experience in your Executive Summary.) To make your business seem more substantial, add the names and credentials of key advisors, such as your attorney or accountant.

■ Highlight your key team members

This section describes the people who run your business. Develop brief summaries to explain their current roles and highlight their qualifications, past experience, education, and other characteristics, particularly as they relate to those roles. Your goal is to demonstrate that you have brought together the right team to make your company successful.

Begin with the founder, usually viewed as the most important person in the company. Founders often serve as the top managers, exercising day-to-day control over business operations. Then list and briefly describe the other key members of your management team.

Other key roles include:

- **Top decision makers:** President, chief executive officer, division president

- **Operations:** Chief operating officer, plant or production manager

- **Technology:** Chief technology officer, MIS director

- **Marketing and sales:** Vice president of marketing, director of sales

- **Human resources:** HR director, training director

(Note: Founders often fill one or more of the roles listed above.)

If you are creating a business plan primarily to seek funding, limit the number of people you include to the five or six most critical to your long-term success.

As you describe each individual, explain:

- What is their role in the company?

- What past experience or education qualifies them for the job?

- What past successes have they had?

- What are their key professional and personal strengths?

- What (if any) is their personal financial investment in the company?

QUICK**TIP**

Building Your Team

If yours is a young company, don't hire more people than absolutely necessary. Since your income is uncertain, it's better to start small and add staff—whether full-time or part-time—as your business grows. Instead, consider using outside consultants and contractors, even for relatively important tasks. You can outsource all types of responsibilities: sales, marketing, bookkeeping, human resources, and technology. As your revenues increase, you can bring these tasks in house.

Key Team Members

Charlotte Alexander, President. Prior to founding ComputerEase, Charlotte Alexander was the regional vice president for Wait's Electronics Emporium, a computer and electronics retailer with 23 stores in the Midwest. Before that, she was a sales representative with IBM for five years.

Alexander began her association with Wait's Electronics Emporium as manager of the downtown Vespucci store. In her first year, she increased sales by over 42%, in her second year by 39%. She was named "Manager of the Year" for the Wait's chain.

Alexander assumed the role of regional vice president of the Wait's chain three years ago. She was responsible for the company's strategic development for Indiana, Ohio, and Illinois. In that position, Alexander conducted an evaluation of the potential of adding software training to augment the chain's computer hardware sales. This evaluation led Alexander to believe that a substantial need for corporate software training existed but could not be met by an electronics retailer. Instead, a stand-alone operation should be formed. This was the concept behind ComputerEase.

Alexander's association with Wait's Electronics Emporium, coupled with her years at IBM, has given her an extensive background selling technology services and products to large corporations.

Alexander owns 60% of the stock in ComputerEase and serves as Chairman and as Treasurer of the Board of Directors.

Ishaan Permaul, Vice President, Marketing. Ishaan Permaul joined ComputerEase with primary responsibility for the company's marketing and sales activities.

Prior to joining ComputerEase, Permaul served as assistant marketing director for AlwaysHere Health Care Plan. His responsibilities included making direct sales to human resource directors, developing marketing materials and campaigns, and supervising sales personnel. He held that position for seven years prior to joining ComputerEase. Permaul's experience marketing to the human resources community gives him the ideal background for ComputerEase, which sells its services primarily through human resources and training directors.

In previous relevant positions, Permaul was a sales representative for SpeakUp Dictation Equipment, where he sold technological equipment to corporations, and copy editor for the Catchem Advertising Agency.

Permaul owns 10% of the stock in ComputerEase.

Highlights demonstrated success

Related experience

Financial commitment to the company

Experience relates to several aspects of the business

Describe the qualifications of your top-level management. List your key managers' names, job responsibilities, relevant past experience, and other noteworthy attributes.

President/CEO

_____

_____

_____

Key Management: Finance/Administration

_____

_____

_____

Key Management: Operations/Technology

_____

_____

_____

_____

Key Management: Marketing/Sales

_____

_____

_____

_____

Key Management: Human Resources/Personnel

_____

_____

_____

_____

Key Management: Strategy/New Products/Research & Development

_____

_____

_____

_____

■ Predict future management needs

New or changing companies usually have not yet filled all their key management positions. If you are looking for investors or lenders, it's likely that you're going to use some of the funds raised to hire additional leaders. In this section, summarize the roles you need filled and the desired qualifications of the people you hope to bring on board. Questions to consider include:

- What roles in the company will they be filling?

- What experience, qualifications, and education (if job-related) should they have?

- What other characteristics are you looking for in these individuals?

- How will these additional managers help round out your team?

Identify the types of individuals who will complete your team. For example, if your current team has strong marketing experience but less experience in managing money, adding someone with "strong financial management experience" would be a priority in future management hires.

Use the worksheet opposite to summarize the desired qualifications of top team members you plan to hire in the next year or two. Their skills, experience, and personalities should complement those of other top managers and fill any perceived holes.

SAMPLE PLAN:

Future Management Needs

Vice President of Instructional Design (To Be Selected). In the next year, ComputerEase will add a third key management position, Vice President of Instructional Design. The individual selected will have substantial experience designing courseware and running a training organization in a mid- to large-size organization composed of instructional designers, writers, editors, videographers, and instructors. This future vice president will possess outstanding training skills and have experience developing interactive, computer-based training programs. Ideally, he or she will have training experience specifically related to software applications as used in the corporate environment. This person will be tasked with staying abreast of evolving technology and customer demands in the instruction arena, especially in the online environment.

Balances out other team experience

What top management positions are you seeking to fill, or will you need to fill, in the near future? Describe the roles you anticipate and qualifications you'll be looking for in any future management employees. Omit this section if you do not anticipate hiring any additional key management in the next year or two.

1. Key Management to Be Hired

2. Key Management to Be Hired

3. Key Management to Be Hired

■ Describe your staffing structure

Describe the composition of the rest of your staff, the people who carry out the day-to-day work of your company. There's no need to provide the name and qualifications of each individual. Instead, present a general summary of your staffing situation, focusing on job roles, responsibilities, and staff costs. For example, an apparel store might have three salespeople making $12 per hour, plus commission, while a restaurant might include 10 part-time servers, paid a combined $140,000 a year, plus tips.

Use the worksheet opposite to describe the makeup of your staff. Also indicate any expected changes to your staff composition or staffing levels, such as adding additional employees, or plans to outsource responsibilities to independent contractors or consultants.

GO GLOBAL:
Managing International Teams

Unless you have significant international operations, you may not need international management, but the more you operate in other countries, the bigger challenge you face managing that solely domestically. Managing customers, employees, or substantial outsource operations from a great distance can be very difficult, especially if you also have to deal with barriers due to language or culture, or even significant time zone problems. In such cases, you may want to have management or a significant number of employees located in other countries. Typically, the management responsibilities that are most likely to be located abroad include: supervision of technical staff; sales; marketing; customer service; and call center management. And remember, even if you do not actually locate management abroad, you may need locally based management to supervise your internationally based contractors or employees.

Staff Structure

In addition to the two primary managers now on staff and a Vice President of Instructional Design to be hired, ComputerEase currently employs one full-time staff member and contracts for other key services. Additionally, the company hires training course leaders as needed, but they serve as independent contractors.

The full-time staff member is the Office Manager, serving as receptionist, customer service representative, and mail handler. A consultant instructional designer works on developing and updating the courseware, and a contract Web developer created an easy-to-use template for uploading courses to the company's website, reducing the company's need for permanent technical Web staff. Commissioned telesales workers call up prospects and generate leads for Vice President of Marketing Ishaan Permaul and President and CEO Charlotte Alexander to follow up on.

As ComputerEase expands, the company will hire part-time training instructors rather than relying solely on outside contractors. This will reduce costs, but just as important will ensure greater consistency in the quality of the company's offerings.

Staff to be hired in the future

What are the jobs of employees on your staff? List them here, along with the number of people who fill those roles, and their pay rate/range.

Job Role	Number of Employees in Role	Pay Rate/Range

What staff will you add in the near future?

Identify your board members, advisors, and consultants

It is often a good idea—and sometimes a legal necessity—to turn outside your company for additional guidance and advice. If you have formal outside relationships, such as with the members of a board of directors, include the names and brief biographies of members in your business plan. For informal relationships, such as those with advisory committees or consultants, include information about them if they add credibility or stature to your company.

Key outside advisors include:

Board of Directors. Boards of directors typically have legal responsibility for a company. If your company is incorporated, you're almost certainly required by law to have a board of directors. In startups, this may consist of only one person: the founder. In larger companies or companies with investors, the board usually consists of individuals with a financial stake in the company and, possibly, additional members knowledgeable about the industry. Venture capitalists generally require board membership as a condition of their investment.

Advisory Committee. Advisory committees do not have legal responsibility for a company. Thus, it is possible to identify a range of individuals whose ongoing expertise and advice you'd like to have for your company. Advisory committees can be very informal, and may meet infrequently, but they give you a way to ask people you respect to assist you in building your company.

Consultants and Other Professionals. Almost all new and expanding businesses rely on consultants to provide critical guidance and professional services. Include these in your plan *only* if they play a key role or if their names will add luster to your business plan. Such consultants include:

- Attorneys
- Accountants
- Management consultants
- Marketing consultants
- Industry specialists
- Technology advisors

SAMPLE PLAN:

Board Members, Advisors, and Consultants

BOARD OF DIRECTORS

Charlotte Alexander is the Chairman of the Board and Treasurer.

Cathy J. Dobbs, the company's attorney (and founder of the firm Dobbs, Kaye, and Babbitt) serves as Secretary.

The position of Vice Chairman has been reserved for an outside investor.

Board consists of founder and outside professional advisor

ADVISORY COMMITTEE

An informal advisory committee provides guidance to the officers and staff of ComputerEase. The committee meets quarterly, and members of the committee are available as resources to the company on an ongoing basis. The members represent professionals from industries directly related to ComputerEase's mission and target market.

Members of the committee:

Joe Chow, Director of Human Resources, RockSolid Insurance Company

Justin Glen, Director of Training, Vespucci National Bank

Michelle Wheaton, Marketing Director, SANE Software

Dr. A. A. Arnold, Professor of Instructional Media, Vespucci State University

How committee serves the company

CONSULTANT

A.A. Arnold, Ph.D. Dr. A. A. Arnold, Professor of Instructional Media at Vespucci State University (VSU), serves the company as a consultant in the conception and development of training manuals. A specialist in the design of instructional materials, Dr. Arnold received his Ph.D. in Education with an emphasis on interactive computer-aided training. Currently, Dr. Arnold designs training programs for industry in addition to holding his position at VSU.

Outside consultant gives added credibility

Do you have a board of directors? If so, who are the members? List them here, along with brief biographies, including their professional expertise, financial stake, and compensation (if any).

If you have an advisory committee, who are the members? List them here, along with their professional affiliation, expertise, value to your company, and compensation (if any).

Do you use consultants? List them here, including the names of their firms, areas of expertise, and the ways in which they serve your company.

■ Pulling it all together: Management Structure

Use the worksheet below to prepare the management section of your plan. If yours is a large company, add an organization chart to illustrate how your company is structured.

Conclusion

The success of your business depends on the people who run it. It takes capable people—with appropriate experience and abilities—to build and run a thriving company. Thus, it is no surprise that lenders and investors often turn first to the Management section of a business plan. They want to make certain the people in charge have the background necessary to manage the company.

Who are the key people on your management team? (See worksheet on page 99.)

_____

_____

_____

What management positions do you need to fill in the near future? (See worksheet on page 101.)

_____

_____

_____

What is the makeup of the rest of your staff? (See worksheet on page 103.)

_____

_____

_____

Who are the members of your board of directors and advisory committee, and who are your consultants? (See worksheet on page 105.)

_____

_____

_____

_____

8

Accomplishments

In this step you'll:

☐ Define your long-term goals

☐ Establish future milestones

☐ Assess the risks

☐ Explore exit options

☐ Pulling it all together: Future Development

Time-Saving Tools

You'll complete this section more quickly if you have any of the following handy:

☐ Existing plans for company development

☐ Calendar of planned product releases or expansion activities

Step  8

Future Development

Since a business plan is a road map for your company, you—and those who review your plan—need a clear sense of your ultimate destination. In this section, you'll outline your long-term goals, indicating the milestones you plan to reach along the way. By developing specific objectives, you'll have signposts to measure progress as you go.

If you're seeking investors for your business, this section will be of particular interest to them. When they invest money in your company, they want to assess exactly how much they might gain eventually and how big your company might become. Only then can they understand the potential return on their investment.

It's also important, to both you and your investors, to spell out what might ultimately become of the company. How will you (and any investors) get your investments—and rewards—out of the company in the long term? Even if you're just starting your business, you'll find that considering possible exit strategies changes the way you think about your company and gives you a framework for business planning.

Finally, don't be afraid to look at the risks involved in your business. An honest assessment of risk isn't likely to frighten experienced investors or lenders. They understand that all ventures involve some risk; they'll respect the fact that you understand and anticipate the risks involved.

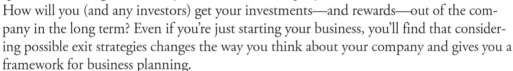 **KEY TO SUCCESS**

Tailor Your Plans to Your Needs

What you include in this section depends on the purpose of your business plan, especially if you are seeking funding. If you're looking for funds to finance growth, this is the place to share your vision. If, on the other hand, you're looking for money to deal with financial difficulties, use this section to explain the changes you'll be making to improve your company's health.

■ Define your long-term goals

What do you expect your company to look like in one year? Five years? Ten years? In this section, describe your long-term vision and plans. Be as specific as you can, focusing on issues such as:

- Sales levels

- Profit levels/margins

- Number of employees

- Number of locations

- Number of product(s)/product lines

- Market share

For example, a small accounting office might have the goal of securing 20 new corporate clients in the next year, adding two additional accountants and a bookkeeping service over the next three years, and opening a second location within the next five years.

Qualitative versus Quantitative Goals

If you have not yet determined specific, quantitative goals—the kind with numbers attached—include any other goals you have for your company. Even though these may be less specific than sales or profit goals, they still give an indication of the direction you plan for your business. Such qualitative goals include: dominating a niche market, penetrating a new market, being an industry innovator, or becoming the recognized quality leader.

SAMPLE PLAN:

Long-Term Goals

> Intends to become a market leader, both locally and online

ComputerEase plans to grow steadily over the next five years, becoming a known and respected brand providing software training to large- and medium-size businesses in person and in the online space. Within the next decade, the company will bring in $5 million annually in online sales. In its on-premise business, it will capture a market share of at least 50 percent of all corporate software training (in terms of revenues) in the Greater Vespucci area. Within 10 years, the company plans to have expanded its physical presence throughout the Midwest, with offices in five locations, having captured at least one-third of the share of the corporate software training market in the region, with revenues of $3 million annually. In total, in 10 years the company hopes to reap $8 million annually in sales.

Describe what your company will look like in the future. Be specific about sales levels, products, profit levels, and numbers of employees and locations.

What are the specific goals you have for your company in the next year?

What will your company achieve in the next three to five years?

What will your business look like in 10 years?

QUICK**TIP**

One Thing at a Time

Most entrepreneurs have many good—even great—ideas on how to grow their businesses. But it's easy to get distracted by too many good ideas. Focus on building one aspect of your business at a time. Demonstrate that you can plan, execute, and succeed in one stage of your business before moving on to the next.

■ Establish future milestones

How will you know that you are making progress toward your long-term goals? Milestones will help you measure how far you've come.

Your milestones should be described in specific numerical terms so you'll know if you're making sufficient progress toward your goals. An accounting firm, for instance, could set as a future milestone reaching $650,000 in revenue by the end of the second year, or have a goal of adding 10 new corporate clients in each of the next three years.

Outlining your milestones also serves as a step-by-step guide, showing how you intend to carry out your long-term business development plans. If, for instance, your goal is to reach sales of $3 million by year five, indicate how much you'll need in sales by years two, three, and four. Then, indicate the strategies you'll use to get to those levels. Will you add marketing staff? Start a direct mail campaign? Add locations or product lines?

A milestone list allows you and your investors to see what you plan to accomplish, and it sets out clear objectives. These objectives are an essential part of your business plan.

What Milestones Have You Reached?

Instill confidence in your future prospects by highlighting your past achievements—the milestones you've already reached with your business. Include these past milestones in your Company Description (see page 19). But don't be afraid to repeat them here if they demonstrate that you're likely to reach your future goals, as well. For example, if you've already established strategic partnerships with three industry leaders, that's a good indication you can forge three more, as you've indicated in your future milestones list.

SAMPLE PLAN:

Future Milestones and Development Strategy

To reach the long-term goal of becoming one of the major players in corporate software training in the online world as well as the dominant training provider in the Midwest, ComputerEase will continue to add new courses to its product line and add training classrooms and locations each year.

The first priority is to double the number of products in the company's online course portfolio within the year, and to continually expand it every year. A second priority in that same timeframe is to open the company's second Corporate Training Center in the city of Whitten Park. That location will serve both as an additional training classroom and as a base of additional marketing activities.

In each of the following two years, ComputerEase plans to win at least 10 major new corporate accounts to deliver custom online training on enterprise applications as well as off-the-shelf software. ComputerEase also plans on opening at least one additional company-run Corporate Training Center per year, concentrating on cities within a three-hour drive of Vespucci that have a substantial number of large- and medium-size corporations.

By year three, ComputerEase management will assess future options for growth. Likely scenarios include the addition of more company-run Corporate Training Centers, the possibility of franchising the operation, or of merging with or being acquired by another online training company.

First-year milestone

Describes short-term strategies necessary to meet longer-term goals

Long-term expansion strategies

List the specific accomplishments you'll achieve on the way to your long-term goals. Give numerical objectives—sales and profit figures, number of customers, employees, and locations—and target dates.

Milestone	Level Achieved	Target Date

What specific steps will you take to reach those milestones?

■ Assess the risks

Running a business entails a measure of risk. Even a company with highly qualified management and well-conceived strategies might be affected by outside events.

Some types of risk any company—including yours—faces are:

- **Competitive risk.** Competitors may drive down prices, market their product or service more aggressively, or substantially enhance their offerings; new competitors may enter the field.

- **Market risk.** The economic health, needs, or desires of the target market may change.

- **Operational risk.** Critical aspects of your operations may change—suppliers may go out of business; equipment or technology may change.

- **Financial risk.** The cost of materials, energy, or labor may rise substantially.

- **Execution risk.** You may not be able to achieve the results planned in the time predicted, or you may not be able to manage your growth.

- **Economic risk.** The health of the overall economy may change, or specific financial factors, such as interest rates, may have a negative effect.

- **Global risk.** When doing business internationally, you may encounter unanticipated situations that will interrupt or stop your ability to do business, reach your market, or receive supplies.

In this section, spell out the risks you're most likely to face, along with the steps you'll take to reduce those risks. If you're looking for funding, show investors or lenders that you're realistic about the challenges you could face.

SAMPLE PLAN:

Risk Assessment

Identifies risks from potential competition

ComputerEase faces risks on two fronts. The first is that increased competition in the online training market will become so intense that margins collapse, making it difficult to be profitable given the cost of developing and supporting high-quality courseware. The second is that new on-premises competitors will enter the market from outside the Greater Vespucci area. It is highly likely that existing franchised software training companies from other parts of the country will open franchises in this region. Since these national companies offer financing to their franchisees, the major barrier to entry—the cost of establishing a training center—can be overcome. If the franchisee is highly capable, this represents the greatest risk to ComputerEase.

Strategy for reducing risk

To prepare for both these eventualities, it is critical that ComputerEase quickly and aggressively increase its market share—both in its geographic market and online—and begin building strong brand awareness for its products. Corporate customers are slow to change established vendors, and ComputerEase anticipates that it will be able to retain a high percentage of existing customers, even in the face of new competitors. Moreover, ComputerEase management remains open to the possibility of a merger or other agreement with a national company if that appears to be a better financial option.

Another risk is that market conditions will deteriorate. ComputerEase is highly dependent on the business economy. Companies reducing their training budgets will have a direct negative impact on ComputerEase revenues.

To counteract that, the company is rapidly increasing its marketing to individual consumers—online, in print publications, and in offering Saturday and evening classes. In the face of an economic downturn or layoffs, individuals need to take classes to improve their marketable skills, and this provides some balance to fluctuations in the corporate market.

What are the potential risks facing your company? List them here, along with your plans to minimize them.

Potential Risk	Plan to Reduce Risk

■ Explore exit strategies

If you're just starting your business, it's hard to imagine what might eventually become of your company. But thinking through scenarios of what might ultimately happen to your business is helpful to you, and it's absolutely essential for investors.

An exit strategy gives focus to how you'll build your business. If you'd eventually like to sell your business, you're going to plan your business quite differently than if you'd like to hand it down to your children or have it go public on a stock exchange. See page 118 for more on exit plans.

If there's more than one partner or principal in the business, creating a clear exit strategy reduces the friction that can come from having unspoken assumptions. One founder may dream of building a company worth millions and selling it in a few years, while the other may hope to build a modest company they can run together for many years. Sitting down and clarifying an exit strategy puts both on the same track.

An exit plan is absolutely critical if you're looking for investors. After all, they want to know how they will get their money back. Once you've built up the value of your business, how will that value be converted to cash or easily traded stock?

The Exit Plan

In establishing itself as a market leader, ComputerEase will become a likely target for acquisition by or merger with a national software training company or other national for-profit educational institution. For-profit education companies are among the fastest growing firms in the United States, and they regularly acquire existing training schools as a method of achieving their growth targets.

Moreover, as other software training companies have demonstrated, the ComputerEase concept lends itself well to franchising. Franchising would produce additional revenue streams to the company from the franchisees, both from franchise fees and through the purchase of materials and staff training. If the decision is made to franchise, venture capital investment will be sought. Current investors could choose to liquidate their holdings in ComputerEase at that time or convert their holdings to stock in the franchise operation.

Describe the likely exit strategies for your company. If you're seeking investors, concentrate on strategies enabling you and investors to convert the value of your company to cash or easily traded stock.

Exit Plan Options

OPTION	DESCRIPTION	BENEFITS	DRAWBACKS
Go public	Sell stock in the company on a public stock exchange	The stock easily converts to cash; liquidity	Must be a large company; approx. $25 to $50 million; highly regulated
Acquisition	Another company buys yours	Investors receive cash and/or stock	Must be a good fit for the existing company; company must have clear value
Sale	Individuals buy the company	Investors get cash	Must find a willing buyer; company must have clear value
Merger	Join with an existing company	Investors may receive stock in the new company or some cash	Usually little or no cash; stock may not be easily traded
Buy-Out	One or more current shareholders buy out the interest of another	Sellers get cash	Buyer must have sufficient cash; negotiations often contentious
Franchise	Replicate concept by licensing rights to others	Receive cash; franchisees finance expansion	Concept must be appropriate; legally complicated
Hand-Down	Give company to the next generation	Stays in family	Family tensions; little or no cash; tax implications
Close	End operations	Relatively easy; sense of closure	No financial reward; possible sense of loss

What Is ROI?

One of the most important factors investors consider when deciding whether to finance a company is the potential ROI, or Return on Investment.

ROI is the amount of money an investor gains in return for his/her investment investment. ROI is usually expressed as an annual percentage of the total investment. This figure makes it possible to quickly compare different financial opportunities, such as investing in a specific company versus investing in the stock market. Investors are looking for the largest return on their money, so the higher the ROI, the better.

The basic factors determining an investment's ROI include:

- **All financial costs**—initial investment and any follow-on investments

- **All financial gains**—including both the increase in funds (if any) from the investment and the return of the investors' money

- **Time period**—how long it takes to realize these gains

There may also be nonfinancial benefits of an investment that figure in an investor's decision, such as the satisfaction to be gained from participating in a young company's growth.

Let's say an investor is considering investing in one of two companies:

- **Company A:** A $50,000 investment is projected to return a total of $100,000 to the investor in 2 years.

- **Company B:** A $150,000 investment is projected to return a total of $300,000 to the investor in 4 years.

In both scenarios, the investor doubles their money. So which is the better investment?

An investment in Company B nets the investor a larger monetary gain: $150,000 versus only $50,000 in Company A. *But*, due to the length of time required before the investment in Company B pays off, the simple ROI in Company A is actually higher:

- **Company A:** 200% return in 2 years, or 100% ROI per year

- **Company B:** 200% return in 4 years, or 50% ROI per year

■ Pulling it all together: Future Development

The Development section of your business plan shows you have given careful thought to how your business will grow over time. Present your readers with a clear vision of your future, along with a realistic strategy for getting there. Be sure your plan incorporates well-defined goals, specific milestones, and an honest assessment of risk. And be certain to include an exit plan; demonstrate how you and your investors can eventually recover the investment you've put into your company and convert any increase in value into cash.

What is your long-term goal for your company's future? (See worksheet on page 111.)

_____

_____

_____

_____

What milestones will you reach along the way? (See worksheet on page 113.)

_____

_____

_____

What are the risks involved and how will you minimize those risks? (See worksheet on page 115.)

_____

_____

_____

_____

What are possible exit options? (See worksheet on page 117.)

_____

_____

_____

_____

Accomplishments

In this step you'll:

- ☐ Produce your Income Statement
- ☐ Develop your Cash Flow Projection
- ☐ Generate your Balance Sheet
- ☐ Show your Sources and Use of Funds
- ☐ Consider preparing additional supporting financial statements

Time-Saving Tools

You'll complete this section more quickly if you have any of the following handy:

- ☐ Current and past financial records
- ☐ Historical sales figures
- ☐ Projected costs
- ☐ Payroll numbers
- ☐ Any past loan documents
- ☐ Company tax returns for past years (for an existing company)
- ☐ Sales projections, marketing budget, staffing budget

Financials

People in business fall into one of two categories: those who fear dealing with numbers and those who are fascinated by them. If you're in the first category, the prospect of completing all your financial statements can be intimidating.

Moreover, if you're using your business plan to seek funding, it's daunting to know that investors or lenders often turn to the financials first. That's because your financials give a clear picture of how you earn and spend your money and how big you expect your company to become.

Take heart: numbers are not magical, mysterious, or menacing. They merely reflect the decisions you've made in planning or running your business. If you run ads every week in your local newspaper, there's a number associated with that. If you hire a person to help with shipping, there's a number associated with that, too.

Of course, if yours is an existing—rather than a new—company, you may already have many of these financial documents, or the basis for creating them. Examine your past financial performance and expenses when putting together your future projections, and include historical numbers in your business plan.

KEY TO SUCCESS

Overcoming Finance-Phobia

If you shy away from dealing with numbers, it's easy to get into financial trouble. Learn to pay attention to your ongoing financial situation. It will help you avoid unpleasant surprises. Even if you leave the number-crunching, bill paying, and financial data entry to someone else, familiarize yourself with how to read and understand your financial statements. They'll help you make better business decisions and retain more control over your operations.

The Most Important Financial Statements

The four most important financial statements to include in your business plan are:

1. Income Statement. Shows whether your business is profitable (this is also called a Profit & Loss statement or "P&L").

2. Cash Flow Projection. Indicates whether you'll have enough money to pay your bills.

3. Balance Sheet. Shows the value of your company—your total assets and liabilities.

And, if you're seeking financing:

4. Sources and Use of Funds. Explains where the money you need to run your business will come from (including your own pocket) and the major ways you intend to use it.

These four financial statements act as a summary of your entire financial picture, and they may be the only financial statements you need to include with your business plan, especially if yours is a simple business.

However, before preparing these four major financial statements, you'll find it helpful to produce the following:

- **Sales Projections:** Estimates your levels of sales and revenues in specific time periods.

- **Marketing Budget:** Details how much money you'll spend on all your marketing activities: advertising, trade shows, sales materials, and so on.

- **Staffing Budget:** Outlines your staffing levels, staff positions, and costs.

See page 148 for more information on these three additional forms.

Time Periods to Cover

Some investors or lenders will tell you the time periods they want your financial statements to cover. If they don't, here are typical guidelines for:

New businesses: One to three years. First year, monthly projections; years two and three, quarterly projections.

Existing businesses: Same as for new businesses *plus* historical financial records from the past three to five years.

Businesses seeking venture capital: Five-year projections. First one to two years, monthly; years two and three, quarterly; years four and five, annual projections.

Additional Financials

Depending on the nature of your business (and the demands of your investors or lenders), there are a number of additional financial documents you can choose to include with your business plan, such as:

- **Break-Even Analysis.** Calculates how much you need to make in sales each month before you begin to make a profit.

- **Capital Expenditures.** Details purchases of tangible property, such as facilities, land, equipment, vehicles, and computers. Such purchases have different tax and accounting implications than other expenses.

- **Inventory.** Details the amount you spend or have tied up in inventory.

- **Professional Services Budget.** Is useful for a company that depends heavily on outsourced professionals, including independent contractors, consultants, attorneys, and accountants.

Since most businesses do not need to include these financial statements with their business plans, they are not included here. However, templates for these (and additional financial statements) are included in the Business Plan Financials package available for download purchase at PlanningShop: *www.PlanningShop.com.*

QUICK**TIP**

Hire a Professional

Every business benefits by having access to the services of an accountant or book-keeper, especially in the early stages. Among their many valuable services, they'll help:

- Set up your books

- Assist you in understanding financial terms and legal requirements

- Provide valuable advice on billing, payment, and payroll procedures

- Advise you on tax-saving strategies

- Assist with the financial components of your business plan

■ Produce your Income Statement

Your Income Statement, also referred to as a Profit and Loss (P&L) statement, is the most widely relied upon of your financial statements. It summarizes the amount of money taken in and the amount of money spent over a designated period of time. This summary of revenue and expenditures reveals whether your company is profitable. It is read from top to bottom, with the first line showing total overall sales. Each subsequent line shows expenses that are deducted from your income until you get to the number at the end representing your profit or loss: your "bottom line."

To prepare your Income Statement, gather detailed information about your sales and expenses. Feel free to change the terms or language on the specific lines—especially in the expenses section—to mirror the categories you use to maintain your own accounts. Using the worksheet on pages 132-133, compile your pro forma (projected) Income Statements on a month-by-month basis. Use the same line items to produce annual or quarterly Income Statements. If yours is an existing business, use the same form for your historical Income Statements.

Your Income Statement provides the quickest overview of your company's profitability. Investors and lenders are naturally interested to know when you're going to be profitable and how much money you'll be making.

In addition to a month-by-month Income Statement for the current or coming year, include projections for the next few years. On the pages that follow are two sample Income Statements: a month-by-month Income Statement for the fictional company ComputerEase's first year in business (pages 128-129) and a three-year projection compiled on an annual basis (page 130).

Income Statement Terms

Additional terms are defined in the *Business Terms Glossary* included on pages 183-184.

- **Gross Sales:** Total sales from all product line categories before *any* costs.

- **Allowances:** Amounts deducted from invoices for reasons such as buyer's speedy payment, large-quantity purchases, or acceptance of faulty merchandise.

QUICK**TIP**

Measuring Profitability

While an Income Statement is a reflection of a company's profit, it doesn't present the complete financial picture. For example, a business that's losing money on an annual basis could still be worth quite a lot because it owns valuable property—and that will show up on the Balance Sheet. On the other hand, a profitable company may not have the cash flow to pay the bills. An Income Statement doesn't reveal either of these conditions.

- **Net Sales:** Amount of total sales after deducting sales commissions, returns, and allowances.

- **Cost of Goods (COG):** Costs of raw materials, inventory, or other expenses directly associated with producing the product/service for sale.

- **Gross Profit:** Amount of sales after deducting commissions, returns, allowances, and cost of goods.

- **Depreciation:** Not a cash expenditure, but the amount allowed for tax purposes for the cost of ongoing wear-and-tear of fixed assets (facilities and equipment).

- **Net Income:** Amount of income after deducting all costs of doing business.

- **Net Profit:** Amount of income after deducting all costs *plus* taxes.

Income Statement Year: 2021 (Actual through 8/31/21, projected 9-12/21)

	JAN	FEB	MARCH	APRIL	MAY
INCOME					
Gross Sales	$0	$4,000	$4,000	$10,000	$24,000
(Commissions)	0	0	0	0	700
(Returns and allowances)	0	0	0	0	0
Net Sales	0	4,000	4,000	10,000	23,300
(Cost of goods)	0	648	648	1,624	3,892
GROSS PROFIT	0	3,352	3,352	8,376	19,408
EXPENSES — General and Administrative					
Salaries and wages	5,000	7,400	11,400	12,400	15,400
Employee benefits	550	550	1,020	1,020	1,020
Payroll taxes	420	620	1,010	1,010	1,010
Professional services	5,000	500	4,000	400	400
Marketing and advertising	6,400	3,600	8,000	3,000	3,000
Rent	0	0	0	0	0
Equipment rental	500	500	500	500	500
Maintenance	0	0	0	0	0
Depreciation	4,000	0	0	0	0
Insurance	800	0	0	400	0
Telecommunications	200	100	200	200	240
Utilities	500	120	250	420	320
Office supplies	900	250	430	370	250
Postage and shipping	420	160	620	130	900
Travel	110	300	200	300	0
Entertainment	0	0	220	640	390
Interest on loans	0	250	250	250	250
Other: Technology	6,000	0	0	0	0
Other: Furniture	0	0	0	820	0
TOTAL EXPENSES	30,800	14,350	28,100	21,860	23,680
Net income before taxes	(30,800)	(10,998)	(24,748)	(13,484)	(4,272)
Provision for taxes on income	0	0	0	0	0
NET PROFIT	(30,800)	(10,998)	(24,748)	(13,484)	(4,272)

JUNE	JULY	AUG	SEPT	OCT	NOV	DEC	TOTAL
$32,000	**$41,000**	**$56,000**	**$68,400**	**$83,600**	**$100,000**	**$43,000**	**$466,000**
1,500	1,550	2,470	3,000	3,700	4,400	1,900	$19,220
0	0	0	0	0	0	0	$0
30,500	**39,450**	**53,530**	**65,400**	**79,900**	**95,600**	**41,100**	**$446,780**
5,190	6,898	9,482	11,382	13,852	16,800	7,324	$77,740
25,310	**32,552**	**44,048**	**54,018**	**66,048**	**78,800**	**33,776**	**$369,040**
16,800	12,600	19,800	18,200	20,200	22,200	16,600	$178,000
1,020	1,020	1,400	1,400	1,400	1,400	1,400	$13,200
1,010	1,010	1,220	1,220	1,220	1,220	1,220	$12,190
400	400	2,400	400	400	400	400	$15,100
600	3,000	3,500	4,000	500	4,000	500	$40,100
0	0	4,200	4,200	4,200	4,200	4,200	$21,000
500	500	4,000	4,000	4,000	4,000	4,000	$23,500
0	0	240	240	240	240	240	$1,200
0	0	0	0	0	0	0	$4,000
0	400	2,000	700	1,100	700	700	$6,800
260	200	500	400	400	400	400	$3,500
400	350	520	440	420	360	300	$4,400
170	220	2,200	500	500	500	500	$6,790
170	520	120	820	150	600	400	$5,010
50	200	0	300	300	300	300	$2,360
400	150	170	100	100	100	100	$2,370
250	250	250	250	250	250	250	$2,750
6,000	0	0	0	0	0	0	$12,000
0	0	0	0	0	0	0	$820
28,030	**20,820**	**42,520**	**37,170**	**35,380**	**40,870**	**31,510**	**$355,090**
(2,720)	11,732	1,528	16,848	30,668	37,930	2,266	$13,950
0	0	0	0	0	0	2,092	$2,092
(2,720)	**11,732**	**1,528**	**16,848**	**30,668**	**37,930**	**174**	**$11,858**

Income Statement—Three-Year Projection

	2021	2022	2023
INCOME			
Gross Sales	$466,000	$987,750	$1,637,230
(Commissions)	19,220	122,720	165,840
(Returns and allowances)	0	0	0
Net Sales	446,780	865,030	1,471,390
(Cost of goods)	77,740	124,266	173,220
GROSS PROFIT	369,040	740,764	1,298,170
EXPENSES — General and Administrative			
Salaries and wages	178,000	353,600	453,200
Employee benefits	13,200	30,000	43,200
Payroll taxes	12,190	30,000	40,000
Professional services	15,100	10,000	12,000
Marketing and advertising	40,100	60,000	90,000
Rent	21,000	78,000	78,000
Equipment rental	23,500	76,000	96,000
Maintenance	1,200	4,800	9,000
Depreciation	4,000	8,000	8,000
Insurance	6,800	8,400	11,000
Telecommunications	3,500	3,600	4,000
Utilities	4,400	10,000	11,000
Office supplies	6,790	10,000	12,000
Postage and shipping	5,010	7,200	10,000
Travel	2,360	5,190	9,140
Entertainment	2,370	3,610	6,860
Interest on loans	2,750	3,000	0
Other: Technology	12,000	20,000	28,000
Other: Furniture	820	1,000	0
TOTAL EXPENSES	355,090	722,400	921,400
Net income before taxes	13,950	18,364	376,770
Provision for taxes on income	2,092	2,754	113,440
NET PROFIT	11,858	15,610	263,330

Get your plan *FINISHED FASTER* with
Business Plan Financials

Designed from the ground up to work hand-in-hand with PlanningShop books.

Worksheets are identical to the financial worksheets found in *Successful Business Plan, Business Plan In A Day,* and *Entrepreneurship: A Real-World Approach*—no new formats to wrestle with!

All the math and calculations are done for you!

"Help Balloons" provide convenient information and advice.

Built on Microsoft Excel, the powerful industry standard for generating compelling financial reports.

Fill out the information in one worksheet and it automatically transfers to other appropriate worksheets.

Charts and graphs are automatically generated for you!

When you're finished, just print out your Income Statement, Cash Flow Projections, and Balance Sheets and add them to your plan.

DESIGNED FOR READERS OF PLANNINGSHOP BOOKS!

Easily complete the financial worksheets for your business plan on your computer! This Excel-based package of financial statements matches the financial worksheets in PlanningShop books.

TRUE "FLOW-THROUGH FINANCIALS"

Now you can enter your financial figures just once, and they'll automatically flow through to all your other relevant financial statements, performing necessary calculations along the way!

Compatible with both Mac and Windows.

Download your copy today:
www.PlanningShop.com

INCOME STATEMENT					
	Jan	Feb	March	April	May
For Year _____					
INCOME					
Gross Sales					
(Commissions)					
(Returns and allowances)					
Net Sales					
(Cost of goods)					
GROSS PROFIT					
OPERATING EXPENSES					
General and Administrative Expenses					
Salaries and wages					
Employee benefits					
Payroll taxes					
Professional services					
Marketing and advertising					
Rent					
Equipment rental					
Maintenance					
Depreciation					
Insurance					
Telecommunications					
Utilities					
Office supplies					
Postage and shipping					
Travel					
Entertainment					
Interest on loans					
Other:					
Other:					
TOTAL OPERATING EXPENSES					
Net income before taxes					
Provision for taxes on income					
NET PROFIT AFTER TAXES					

June	July	Aug	Sept	Oct	Nov	Dec	TOTAL

■ Develop your Cash Flow Projection

On a day-to-day basis, your Cash Flow Projection is your most important financial analysis. It shows how much money you have coming into your business and how much going out. This "flow" indicates whether you'll have enough cash to pay your bills.

The Cash Flow Projection is not about profit—that shows up on the Income Statement. And it's not about the overall value of your company—that appears on the Balance Sheet. It's about how much money you have in the bank. It's a real-life picture of your cash situation.

Cash Flow Projections are particularly important for seasonal businesses, those with large inventories, and businesses that sell primarily on credit. You must plan for the lag time between buying materials, making sales, and actually receiving cash.

In preparing Cash Flow Projections, existing businesses should review past financial records to determine actual income and expense patterns. New businesses can check with others in their industry to gauge typical payment patterns.

A sample Cash Flow Projection appears on pages 136-137. Fill out the worksheet on pages 138-139 to project your company's cash flow.

The Cash Crunch

Even profitable businesses can easily get into a cash crunch, so keep an eye on your bank balance. Many businesses—especially growing ones—spend more than they receive on a month-by-month basis. After all, you typically have to pay for raw materials months before you're going to receive payment for the finished product. This delay presents a tricky problem for entrepreneurs, and most businesses use lines of credit or other financing tools to manage their cash flow needs.

Cash Flow Terms

- **Cash Sales:** Sales made where the income is received immediately. These can include credit card sales because the revenue is deposited in the company's bank within days.

- **Collections:** Income collected from accounts receivable—sales made on credit in a previous period.

- **Interest Income:** Cash received from interest-bearing accounts, such as certificates of deposit or interest on accounts receivable.

- **Loan Proceeds:** Cash received as a result of taking out a loan, a credit card advance, or using another credit line.

- **Equity Capital Investments:** Cash received from investors in return for a share of ownership (equity).

- **Owner's Draw:** Money paid to owner instead of (or in addition to) a salary.

- **Opening Cash Balance:** The amount of money in the bank or account at the beginning of the period (month, year, or quarter)—the same as the previous period's Ending Cash Balance.

Cash Is King

The following methods help improve your cash flow:

- **Sell sooner.** Sell your product or service before you actually fulfill the order, through pre-sales, early season sales, and gift cards.

- **Get paid faster.** Make it as easy as possible for customers to pay you. Accept credit cards and mobile payments, and send out your invoices as soon as possible.

- **Reduce costs and waste.** Forecast what you need and purchase carefully. If you don't need it, don't buy it, whether it's extra inventory, shipping materials, utilities, or trips in your van.

- **Defer payments.** Negotiate payment terms, ask for payment installments, or pay bills with a credit card. If you sell online, arrange for a vendor to directly fulfill your customer orders—you hold little or no inventory, and receive cash before you make the expenditure.

Cash Flow Projection Year: 2021

	JAN	FEB	MARCH	APRIL	MAY
CASH RECEIPTS					
Income from Sales					
Cash sales	$0	$4,000	$4,000	$10,000	$24,000
Collections	0	0	0	0	0
Total Cash from Sales	0	4,000	4,000	10,000	24,000
Income from Financing					
Interest income	0	0	0	0	0
Loan proceeds	30,000	0	0	12,000	20,000
Equity capital investments	40,000	0	20,000	0	0
Total Cash from Financing	70,000	0	20,000	12,000	20,000
Other cash receipts	0	0	0	0	0
TOTAL CASH RECEIPTS	70,000	4,000	24,000	22,000	44,000
CASH DISBURSEMENTS					
Expenses					
Inventory	0	648	648	1,624	3,892
Operating Expenses	30,800	14,350	28,100	21,860	23,680
Commissions/Returns & Allowances	0	0	0	0	700
Capital Purchases	20,000	0	0	0	0
Loan Payments	0	250	250	250	250
Income tax payments	0	0	0	0	0
Investor dividend payments	0	0	0	0	0
Owner's draw	0	0	0	0	0
TOTAL CASH DISBURSEMENTS	50,800	15,248	28,998	23,734	28,522
NET CASH FLOW	19,200	(11,248)	(4,998)	(1,734)	15,478
Opening cash balance	0	19,200	7,952	2,954	1,220
Cash receipts	70,000	4,000	24,000	22,000	44,000
Cash disbursements	(50,800)	(15,248)	(28,998)	(23,734)	(28,522)
ENDING CASH BALANCE	19,200	7,952	2,954	1,220	16,698

JUNE	JULY	AUG	SEPT	OCT	NOV	DEC	TOTAL
$24,000	31,000	39,600	40,000	61,600	70,000	31,000	$339,200
8,000	10,000	16,400	28,400	22,000	30,000	12,000	$126,800
32,000	41,000	56,000	68,400	83,600	100,000	43,000	$466,000
0	0	0	0	0	0	0	$0
0	0	8,000	0	0	0	0	$70,000
0	0	0	0	0	0	0	$60,000
0	0	8,000	0	0	0	0	$130,000
32,000	41,000	64,000	68,400	83,600	100,000	43,000	$596,000
0	0	0	0	0	0	0	0
32,000	41,000	64,000	68,400	83,600	100,000	43,000	$596,000
5,190	6,898	9,482	11,382	13,852	16,800	7,324	$77,740
28,030	20,820	42,520	37,170	35,380	40,870	31,510	$355,090
1,500	1,550	2,470	3,000	3,700	4,400	1,900	$19,220
0	0	0	0	0	0	0	$20,000
250	250	250	250	250	10,250	20,250	$32,750
0	0	0	0	0	0	0	$0
0	0	0	0	0	0	0	$0
0	0	0	0	0	5000	5000	$10,000
34,970	29,518	54,722	51,802	53,182	82,320	70,984	$524,800
(2,970)	11,482	9,278	16,598	30,418	17,680	(27,984)	$72,200
16,698	13,728	25,210	34,488	51,086	81,504	99,184	$0
32,000	41,000	64,000	68,400	83,600	100,000	43,000	$596,000
(34,970)	(29,518)	(54,722)	(51,802)	(53,182)	(82,320)	(70,984)	($524,800)
13,728	25,210	34,488	51,086	81,504	99,184	71,200	

CASH FLOW PROJECTION					
	Jan	Feb	March	April	May
For Year _____					
CASH RECEIPTS					
Income from Sales					
Cash Sales					
Collections					
Total Cash from Sales					
Income from Financing					
Interest Income					
Loan Proceeds					
Equity Capital Investments					
Total Cash from Financing					
Other Cash Receipts					
TOTAL CASH RECEIPTS					
CASH DISBURSEMENTS					
Inventory					
Operating Expenses					
Commissions/Returns & Allowances					
Capital Purchases					
Loan Payments					
Income Tax Payments					
Investor Dividend Payments					
Owner's Draw					
TOTAL CASH DISBURSEMENTS					
NET CASH FLOW					
Opening Cash Balance					
Cash Receipts					
Cash Disbursements					
ENDING CASH BALANCE					

CASH FLOW PROJECTION							
June	July	Aug	Sept	Oct	Nov	Dec	TOTAL

■ Generate your Balance Sheet

If you're new to business, the Balance Sheet is likely the most perplexing of the major financial statements. It measures the overall value of your company at a particular time, but this can seem far less tangible than your profits (seen in your Income Statement) or actual cash (appearing in your Cash Flow Projection).

The Balance Sheet itself is divided into two parts:

- The top part, where you list all your assets, such as cash, inventory, real estate, equipment, vehicles, and accounts receivable.

- The bottom part, where you total your liabilities, including accounts payable, loans, and payroll. The remaining amount (if any) is figured to be the *net worth*, expressed as shareholders' equity or retained earnings.

The final amounts for each part should be exactly equal—or *balance*.

The Balance Sheet presents investors and lenders with a snapshot of how much your company is worth, especially if it had to be sold. It shows the value of all tangible property and the extent of all debt. The value of some companies' assets may far exceed their profits, while other companies may show a profit but have heavy long-term debt.

A sample Balance Sheet appears on page 142. Use the worksheet on page 143 to create a balance sheet for your company.

Balance-Sheet Terms

- **Current Assets:** Anything your company has that can be turned into cash relatively quickly, including accounts receivable, inventory, and cash itself.

- **Fixed Assets:** Any tangible property your company owns that could be turned into cash more slowly, including real estate, equipment, and vehicles.

- **Current Liabilities:** Any accounts payable or other bills, debts, or financial obligations that must be paid relatively soon.

- **Long Term Liabilities:** Any financial obligations that must be paid over time, such as mortgages, loans, and equipment loans.

- **Net Worth:** The value of the company after deducting all liabilities from all assets.

- **Paid-In Capital:** Capital received from investors, as opposed to capital generated by the operations of a company.

Balance Sheet

For ComputerEase, Inc.
For Year Ending: December 31, 2021

ASSETS
Current Assets

Cash	$71,200	
Accounts receivable	34,400	
Inventory	4,200	
Other current assets	1,560	
Total Current Assets		**$111,360**

Fixed Assets

Land	0	
Facilities	0	
Equipment	20,000	
Computers & telecommunications	0	
Less accumulated depreciation	(4,000)	
Total Fixed Assets		**$16,000**
Other Assets		0
TOTAL ASSETS		**$127,360**

LIABILITIES
Current Liabilities

Short-term notes payable	27,350	
Income taxes due	6,100	
Other current liabilities	590	
Total Current Liabilities		**$34,040**

Long-Term Liabilities

Long-term notes payable	30,000	
Other long-term liabilities	0	
Total Long-Term Liabilities		**$30,000**

Net Worth

Shareholders' equity	63,320	
Retained earnings	0	
Total Net Worth		**$63,320**
TOTAL LIABILITIES AND NET WORTH		**$127,360**

BALANCE SHEET

Your Company Name

Quarter _____ Year _____

ASSETS

Current Assets

Cash _____

Accounts receivable _____

Inventory _____

Other current assets _____

Total Current Assets _____

Fixed Assets

Land _____

Facilities _____

Equipment _____

Computers & telecommunications _____

    (less accumulated depreciation) _____

Total Fixed Assets _____

Other Assets _____

TOTAL ASSETS _____

LIABILITIES

Current Liabilities

Short-term notes payable _____

Income taxes due _____

Other current liabilities _____

Total Current Liabilities _____

Long-Term Liabilities

Long-term notes payable _____

Other long-term liabilities _____

Total Long-Term Liabilities _____

NET WORTH

Paid-in capital _____

Retained earnings _____

Total Net Worth _____

TOTAL LIABILITIES AND NET WORTH _____

QUICK**TIP**

Accentuate Growth

Financing sources generally prefer to fund companies that are planning to use their newly acquired money for growth rather than to pay off old bills. After all, if you're in financial hot water now, what's to keep you from getting in trouble again? They also like to know they're not the only ones who believe in your business. So, if you can, it's important to:

- Demonstrate you are using funds to start or expand a business

- Indicate you already have commitments from other respected sources

- Show that the owners are committing their own funds as well

■ Show your Sources and Use of Funds

If you are seeking outside financing—loans or investments—you'll need to prepare one more key financial document: the Sources and Use of Funds statement. Your financing sources naturally want to know how much money you need, where you plan to get it, and what you're going to do with the money you raise. They also want to see if you've contributed any of your own money.

The Sources and Use of Funds statement can be a relatively simple one-page (or less) listing. See the sample form on page 146. Your task here is to assure investors and lenders that:

- You have specific plans for the money you raise

- They are aware of all the sources of funds you're seeking or have received

- You are not thoughtlessly taking on debt or giving up equity

- Ideally, you are using the money to help your business grow

Use the worksheet on page 147 to create a Sources and Use of Funds statement.

Sources and Use of Funds Terms

- **Equity Financing:** Money raised from investors who receive a share of the company's ownership in return for their funds.

- **Debt Financing:** Money raised by taking on loans, leases, mortgages, or other financial obligations. Funders receive additional interest payments as well as return of their initial capital in exchange for their funds.

- **Capital Expenditures:** Purchase of tangible property, such as real estate, equipment, and vehicles.

- **Working Capital:** Funds used for ongoing operating expenses of the business, including payroll, administrative and operating expenses, and marketing.

Sources and Use of Funds

Note: The total amount of financing being sought is $160,000 in equity financing. The company prefers that this entire amount be secured from only one investor. It is expected that these funds will be received and expended in early 2022.

SOURCES OF FUNDS

Equity Investment $160,000

USE OF FUNDS

Capital Expenditures

Leasehold Improvements	$10,000
Purchase of Equipment and Furniture	30,000
Total Capital Expenditures	**40,000**

Working Capital

Purchase of Inventory	10,000
Staff Expansion	50,000
Additional Marketing Activities	30,000
Other Business Expansion Activities	30,000
Total Working Capital	**120,000**

TOTAL USE OF FUNDS   **$160,000**

Answer the questions below to develop your "Sources and Use of Funds" statement.

SOURCES OF FUNDS

What is the total amount of financing you are seeking (investments and loans)?

How much are the principals investing?

How much will be in the form of equity investment from others?

How much will be in the form of debt financing, specifically bank loans?

What other forms of debt financing will you be seeking? (Include equipment, mortgage, and vehicle loans/leases.)

What other sources of funds are you seeking, if any?

USE OF FUNDS

How much are you going to spend on capital expenditures (such as real estate, equipment, or computers)? Specify use and cost.

How much are you going to spend on inventory?

How much are you going to spend on working capital to run your business (for example, marketing, staff, and operating expenses)?

■ Consider preparing additional supporting financial statements

Before you develop the four key financial statements, you may find it very helpful to create separate forecasts for a few major components of your income and expenses. If you're using your business plan for internal company planning, these planning tools are particularly useful.

If you're developing your business plan primarily to seek outside financing, you don't necessarily need to prepare these statements. However, doing so will help you find the numbers you need to put in your Income Statement and your Cash Flow Projection.

All of these supporting financial statements, and others, are included in the Business Plan Financials available for download purchase at PlanningShop's website: *www.PlanningShop.com*.

Sales Projections

How many sales are you going to make? When? For how much? Forecasting your sales is obviously critical for understanding how much money you're going to have. Break down your projected sales by product line, on a month-by-month basis. Indicate how much you're going to pay in sales commissions, figure an amount for returns and discounts, and then calculate the cost of goods. This gives you revenue numbers to put in your Income Statement.

Staffing Budget

In many companies, the single biggest expense is the cost of employees. But it's often very frustrating (especially to investors) to see just one big number on the "Salaries" line of a financial statement. Instead, it's helpful to break down your personnel costs by category (management, production, administrative, and marketing, for example), indicating how many employees you'll have in each category and what they'll cost. This also gives you numbers to put in both your Income Statement and your Cash Flow Projection.

Marketing Budget

If marketing is a major expense for your company, you may want to itemize how you plan on spending your marketing and advertising dollars. This budget can be helpful to you in your own internal planning even if you don't include it with the business plan you prepare for outside investors or lenders.

Your financial forms are a critical part of your business plan. Investors and lenders will turn to your financial statements quickly to measure your company's profitability and to see how you earn and spend your money. The four most important financial documents are your Income Statement, Cash Flow Projection, Balance Sheet, and, if you're seeking financing, your Sources and Use of Funds statement. If you're unfamiliar—or uncomfortable—with preparing financial forms, get assistance from an accountant or bookkeeper.

GO GLOBAL:
Financial Considerations

Whenever you cross a country border, you cross financial borders as well. Doing business internationally, you are going to encounter a number of financially related issues that you must keep in mind and plan for. These include:

- Foreign currency exchange
- Currency fluctuations
- Differing standard payment terms
- Differing finance laws and terms
- Additional taxes or tariffs
- Customs charges

- Banking costs and practices
- Interest rates
- Security of funds in financial institutions
- Potential inflation
- Any other international financial variables

Consider all these factors when pricing your products or services internationally, establishing credit policies and charges, and determining where to keep funds and how much to keep overseas.

Sources of Money

SOURCES OF DEBT FINANCING

	WHAT THEY LOOK FOR	ADVANTAGES	DISADVANTAGES
Banks and Lending Institutions	Ability to repay; collateral; steady current income from business	No dilution of your ownership; no profit-sharing; no obligation for ongoing relationship after repayment; definite preset amount to repay **Best For:** Established companies; funding fixed assets, such as property; short-term cash flow management	Difficult to secure for new businesses; must often risk personal assets; financial obligation regardless of business's success **Worst For:** Highly risky ventures and new companies lacking assets
Loans from Family or Friends	Your personal character; other personal considerations; likelihood of repayment	Easier to secure than institutional loans; specific amount to repay; no dilution of ownership or profit-sharing **Best For:** Companies with no other option; companies with a very secure future	Jeopardizing personal relationships; nervous lenders; unsolicited advice and frequent queries **Worst For:** Very risky enterprises; entrepreneurs with difficult family circumstances
Credit Cards, Including Cash Advances	Personal credit score	Relatively easy to secure; immediately available **Best For:** Businesses requiring small amounts of money for a limited time; short-term cash-flow management	Very high interest rates; limited amount of money; ties up and risks personal credit **Worst For:** Ongoing, long-term financing

SOURCES OF EQUITY FINANCING

	WHAT THEY LOOK FOR	ADVANTAGES	DISADVANTAGES
Venture Capitalists	Businesses in their area of interest; companies with high growth potential; experienced management; new technology	Large sums available; sophisticated investors familiar with industry; bring expertise, connections, and future funding; understand business setbacks and capital risk **Best For:** Potentially very large companies; sophisticated entrepreneur or industry wizard	Difficult to secure; must have exit possibilities in 3 to 7 years; take substantial equity in company; may oust founders **Worst For:** Small and medium-size businesses; inexperienced entrepreneurs
Private (Angel) Investors	Good business opportunities with better potential rewards than other investments; appealing concept	Interested in startups; easier to secure than professional venture capital; may have industry knowledge or contacts **Best For:** Companies with high growth potential; companies with appealing business concept	May be involved in decision-making without adequate expertise; long-term relationship; may expect profits soon **Worst For:** Companies requiring extremely long development time before profitability or exit; companies with limited growth potential
Investment from Family and Friends	Interest in you and your business concept; chance to make money	Easier to secure than other investors **Best For:** Companies with no other options; entrepreneurs having friends or relatives with significant business or industry expertise	Jeopardizes personal relationships; long-term involvement; unsophisticated, nervous investors; makes friend or relative a decision-maker in your business **Worst For:** Very risky enterprises; companies requiring long development time before profitability

Whose Money Do You Want?

As you begin your search for financing, ask yourself these questions:

- Are you willing to give up some amount of ownership of your company?

- Are you willing to have debt that you must repay?

- Are you willing to risk property or other assets?

- How much control of the direction and operation of your company are you willing to relinquish?

- What other help do you want from a funder besides money?

- How fast do you want to grow?

- How big do you want your company to be?

- What do you see as the long-term relationship between you and your funding source?

If you're looking for an investor—a venture capitalist (VC) or angel— what will make them actually invest in your company? How will you get them to notice you and convince them that yours is a company they don't want to pass up? Remember that investors see a great many deals. They have a number of other, much safer, options for investing their money.

You're a good catch if investors believe your business will provide them with a high return on the money they invest with you—that is, return on investment, or ROI. The ROI that investing in your business offers has to be higher—much higher—than what an investor could obtain by putting their money into other, less-risky investments, such as stocks, bonds, or real estate.

While investors are comfortable with the amount of risk that is involved in young companies, banks have far different goals and far different purposes. They help companies make large purchases and manage the ups and downs of their cash flow. As a result, they're oriented toward minimizing risk.

No matter how much money you want to borrow, no matter whom you want to borrow money from, the loan process comes down to answering three main questions:

1.   How much money do you need?

2.   What do you need the money for?

3.   Will you pay it back?

Crowdfunding

Crowdfunding is the ability to raise money from a "crowd"—strangers who believe in your idea and are willing to put money into your business. Venture capitalists invest millions, angels invest hundreds of thousands of dollars, and individuals can "invest" small amounts of money through online sites such as Kickstarter to help you get funded.

As with other forms of funding, you'll have to be prepared. As "investors" get more sophisticated, they'll want more than just a great video to motivate them to part with their money. Although the amounts of cash exchanging hands are smaller, you'll still face some of the same scrutiny you would from established investors.

Keys to success in crowdfunding:

- Have a suitable business or product. Consumer, food, consumer electronics, and fashion products are well suited to crowdfunding.
- Create a compelling video. Funders want to hear your story, see you, and view prototypes of your product (if any).
- Have great photos. Pics help supporters spread the word through social media.
- Raise sufficient funds. Make sure you are raising enough to execute on your vision.
- Have a "coolness" factor. Your idea will more likely garner support and go viral if it's unique, attractive, or cutting-edge.
- Plan a marketing campaign. Plan your crowdfunding campaign like you would for any new product.

To search for a crowdfunding platform that meets your needs, check out CrowdsUnite (www. crowdsunite.com).

Presentation Pointers

Looks matter. While your plan will ultimately be judged on the quality of your business concept and your strategies for achieving goals, you also want to make sure it gives the best first impression possible. The way you prepare and present the document is itself an indicator of your professionalism. A polished plan sheds a favorable light on your company; a sloppy or incomplete presentation works against you.

Length of Your Plan

Don't burden your business plan readers with excess verbiage. Keep your business plan as short as is reasonable. Most businesses can keep their plans under 20 pages; those with particularly complex concepts or products should try to limit the plan to 35 pages maximum. Uncomplicated small businesses may not need 20 pages, but anything less than 10 may seem a bit light. You can place additional information in appendices.

12 Critical Slides

Most investors expect to first see your business plan's basic info and highlights in digital form. While there's no exact number that will be right for every business, you should be able to convey all the key details of your company in the following 12 slides.

KEY TO SUCCESS

Break It Up

Large, dense blocks of text intimidate readers. Dividing text with subheads, bullet points, numbers, and white space makes the information on each page more accessible and appealing to your readers. Single space text, but leave an extra line of space between paragraphs.

ComputerEase

SOFTWARE TRAINING SERVICES

Charlotte Alexander
Charlotte@ComputerEase.com
812-555-1234

Title slide: **your company's name, a short company description, name of presenter(s) if presenting in person.**

What We Do

- Business software training services for corporate clients
- Classes conducted on-premise or online
- B2B and B2C target markets
- First 9 months: $171K revenue

ComputerEase

Your elevator pitch: **a succinct description of your products or services, market, and competitive advantages. If possible, embed audio or video to demonstrate your product or service.**

The Opportunity

- Corporate training in No. America = $130 billion industry
- 42% of training outsourced = $54.8 billion
- No market leader
- Huge growth in online training
- Franchise opportunities

ComputerEase

Size of opportunity: **how big your company can potentially grow and what your plans are for future development.**

Your specific target customers: **who they are and the needs that your product or service will meet.**

Target Market

- Corporations with 50+ employees
- Government, insurance, financial, health care, engineering, colleges
- 2,000+ corporations in Vespucci area
- Online market includes U.S. and other English-speaking countries

ComputerEase

The market size: **numbers and dollars, past growth, growth forecasts.**

Market Size

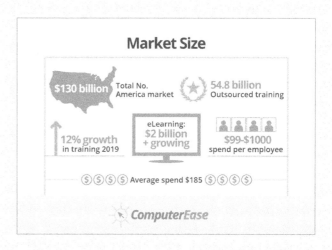

ComputerEase

The competition: **division of market share, how your product compares, your value proposition versus the competition's, and barriers to entry.**

Competition

Current competition:

- Heavily fragmented, no leader
- 3 national training companies
- Online colleges & universities
- Small companies & individual trainers

Competitive advantages:

- Strong team; experienced trainers
- Outstanding training materials
- Corporate market focus
- Certified training

ComputerEase

The Team

Founders:

Charlotte Alexander: President
- Experience selling tech services

Ishaan Permaul: Marketing
- Experience selling to target market

Advisory Committee includes:
- Top customer targets
- Dr. A. A. Arnold, Instructional Design

 ComputerEase

Your team: **who they are, their past successes and experience, and why they are qualified.**

Business Model

- B2B: Top pricing for customized training
- B2C: Top pricing for certification training
- In-house sales team
- Per-seat annual subscription

ComputerEase

The business model: **how you will distribute your product, pricing strategies, how you will reach customers.**

Milestones

- January, 2021 – launched
- August, 2021 – opened first center
- To date:
  - $171k revenue
  - 184 training sessions
  - 11 key corporate clients
- 2023 – second center opens
- 5 years
  - $5 million annual online sales
  - 5 locations
  - $8 million total annual sales

ComputerEase

Milestones: **a time line that outlines when you expect to reach key achievements.**

Financials: **a brief summary of key points from your income statement, balance sheet, and/or cash flow projections.**

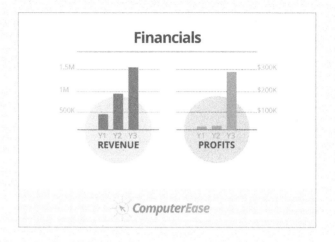

Funding: **amount you are asking for in this round, number of future rounds and their amounts, and how the funds will be used.**

Funding

- Funds sought: $160,000
  - Training Center, staff, marketing
- Funding to date
  - $60K investment – Alexander
  - $70K loans – Alexander/family
- No future funding rounds

ComputerEase

The investment opportunity: **potential exit strategies and financial return for investors.**

The Upside

- High projected annual sales & ongoing profitability
- Proven business concept
- Key customers secured: RockSolid Insurance, Vespucci National Bank, Vespucci State University
- No significant local/regional competition
- Strong potential franchise opportunity

ComputerEase

Format and Layout

- **Choose a clear font.** Pick one that's easy to read and professional in appearance. Generally, serif fonts (the kind with small lines or "feet" at the edges of each letter) make large amounts of text more readable, so choose this style for the body of your plan. Consider Garamond, Palatino, or Times New Roman.

Serif Fonts:

Garamond
Palatino
Times New Roman

Sans serif fonts (those without "feet") work well for headings and subheads, especially in a bold or condensed style. Try Arial, Franklin Gothic, or Verdana.

Sans Serif Fonts:

Arial
Franklin Gothic
Verdana

- **Use no more than two fonts in your plan.** Be restrained in your use of italics, boldface, and underlining. In terms of font size, 10- to 12-point type is best for body text; 12- to 14-point works well for headings and subheads.

Graphs and Charts

As you work on your business plan, look for the kind of information and statistics that you can convey in graphic form, to make a greater impact and keep readers' attention. Even consider "infographics" that display data in interesting fashion. Help your business plan come alive. Place charts of half-page size or less within the text to capture your readers' attention. Produce some or all of your charts or graphs in color for more impact.

Since graphs and charts—especially those in color—attract attention, make certain you include *only* the most important or compelling information in the form of graphs or charts.

Here are some different types of charts you can use to help convey specific information.

FLOW CHARTS

Illustrate development patterns and organization of authority:

Company Work Flow

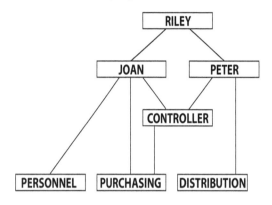

BAR CHARTS

Are useful when demonstrating trends or drawing comparisons:

Purchase of Product , Per Capita by Age Group

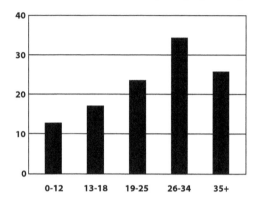

INFOGRAPHICS

Present complex information quickly and clearly in visual form:

Infographic Visual

PIE CHARTS

Are ideal for showing the specific break-downs of products sold, markets, etc.:

Store Sales by Product Category

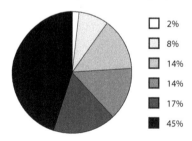

Cover Sheet

Your cover sheet is the first thing readers will see when they open your plan. Make a good first impression with a clean, businesslike design. Your cover sheet should include:

- **Company name.**

- **Company logo**, if you have one.

- The words "**Business Plan**" in a prominent spot.

- The **name, address, phone number, and email address** of the contact person.

- **The date.** To be sure your plan doesn't look outdated, consider including only the year—or create a new cover sheet each time you send out the plan.

- **Copy number.** Number each copy of the plan you send out, and keep track of which reader (or institution) received it.

- **A disclaimer.** If you are circulating your plan to outside funding sources, you need to indicate that the business plan itself is not an offering of stock in the company. A disclaimer can protect you from legal problems and help protect the confidentiality of your plan.

A disclaimer might look like this:

This document is for information only and is not an offering for sale of securities of the Company. Information disclosed herein should be considered proprietary and confidential. The document is the property of _____ Company and may not be disclosed, distributed, or reproduced without the express written permission of _____ Company.

Consult an attorney for proper wording.

Appendix

An appendix allows you to include information at the end of your plan without bogging down the essential sections with too much detail. Some types of information you can include are:

- Positive media coverage

- Letters of intent from potential customers or strategic partners

- List of locations

- Manufacturing descriptions

- Marketing collateral, market research reports, and industry data

- Photos, illustrations, graphs, and charts

- Technical information

Cover Letter

You must include a brief cover letter with any business plan you send or deliver to a potential funding source. Make certain it entices the reader to give careful consideration to your business.

If you send your business plan to someone who has requested it, indicate that fact with a simple sentence, such as:

It was a pleasure meeting you last week. As you requested, I'm sending you a copy of my business plan, for my company, _____.

Then continue to briefly describe your business.

If someone you know is connected to the recipient (an intermediary), start the cover letter with this sentence:

_____ (name of intermediary) suggested that I contact you regarding my business, _____ (name of business), a _____ (type of business).

For example, the first sentence might read:

Phil Turner suggested that I contact you regarding my business, AAA, Inc., a food products and service company.

This draws attention to the person connecting you to the funding source and gives you a measure of credibility.

Next, indicate why you (or the intermediary) feel that the recipient is an appropriate funding source. Continuing with the example above, the next sentence might read:

He knows of your experience in funding food product companies and believes you might find AAA, Inc. of interest.

If you don't have an intermediary and you haven't met the funder yourself, your first sentence should state the name and nature of your company and why you have chosen to send your plan to the recipient. It should read something like:

Knowing of your interest in funding food product companies, I am enclosing a copy of the business plan for AAA, Inc. We are an established food products and service company now seeking financing to enable us to expand operations.

Regardless of how—or how well—you know the recipient of your business plan, your cover letter should state:

- Why you've chosen the particular funder to receive your plan.

- The nature of your business.

- The developmental stage of your business.

- The amount of funds sought.

- Whether you are looking for an investment or a loan.

- The terms of the deal, if appropriate.

Keep your cover letter brief like the sample on the following page.

SAMPLE:

Cover Letter

Ms. Tamara Pinto
617 North Compton Boulevard
Vespucci, Indiana 98999
Charlotte@ComputerEase.com
phone number: 812-555-1234

Dear Ms. Pinto:

My attorney, Mr. Kenneth Pollock, suggested I write to you regarding my business, ComputerEase. I am currently seeking an investor, and I believe that this company would coincide with your interest in technology-related service businesses.

ComputerEase is positioned to take advantage of the market opportunities present in the corporate and consumer software training field. Through a professional approach to marketing, experienced management, and an emphasis on outstanding customer support and service, ComputerEase can become the premier provider of in-person software training in the Greater Vespucci area. From that base, the company will be able to expand to become a regional force. An even greater potential for growth comes from online training, in which no company has yet dominated the market.

We are seeking $160,000. We anticipate this will be the sole round of funding. The funds will be utilized to add one training center location, develop additional courses, expand staff, and increase marketing activities.

I appreciate your consideration of the business plan for ComputerEase. I will telephone in approximately 10 days to see if you have any questions or to discuss how we may proceed.

Thank you.
Sincerely,

Charlotte Alexander
President

A Word about Confidentiality: Nondisclosure Agreements

Although most new entrepreneurs are probably overly concerned about issues of confidentiality, you may want to draw up a "nondisclosure agreement," or NDA, for the recipient to sign before receiving your plan. However, many professional investors—particularly venture capitalists—don't sign NDAs. They see so many plans in so many related industries that they would inevitably have a conflict. See the sample NDA on page 165.

SAMPLE:

NDA

Re: (Company Name)

Nondisclosure Agreement

I agree that any information disclosed to me by _____ Company in connection with my review of the company will be considered proprietary and confidential, including all such information relating to the Company's past, present, or future business activities, research, product design or development, personnel, and business opportunities.

"Confidential Information" means any information disclosed, either directly or indirectly, in writing, orally, or by inspection of tangible objects (including business plans, research, product plans, products, services, customers, markets, software, inventions, processes, designs, drawings, engineering, marketing, or finances).

Confidential Information shall not include information previously known to me or the general public or previously recognized as standard practice in the field. It will also not include information that becomes generally available in the public domain through no action or inaction of myself, my employees, or others associated with me.

I agree not to use any Confidential Information for any purpose except to evaluate and, if applicable, implement a potential business relationship with _____ Company. I agree not to disclose any Confidential Information to third parties or to anyone except those who are required to have the information in order to evaluate or engage in discussions concerning the contemplated business relationship.

I agree that for a period of five years, I will hold all confidential and proprietary information in confidence and will not use such information except as may be authorized by the Company and will prevent its unauthorized dissemination. I acknowledge that unauthorized disclosure could cause irreparable harm and significant injury to the Company. I agree that upon request, I will return all written or descriptive matter, including the business plan and supporting documents, to the Company.

Accepted and Agreed to:

_____

Signature

_____

Printed Name

_____

Company/Title

_____

Date

Final Touches

The best business plans show up on their readers' desks with a clean design; clear, concise content; and an easy-to-navigate structure. Consider these additional guidelines for polishing and packaging your document.

- **Have it edited.** Ask someone with a good command of the English language to edit and proofread your business plan. After developing the plan yourself, you may find it difficult to catch typos and other grammatical problems on your own. You'll also want to see how others interpret your prose.

- **Include a table of contents.** If your plan is longer than 10 pages, include a table of contents to help your readers quickly locate sections that interest them. Place it immediately after your cover sheet and before your Executive Summary.

Sending It Out

Before you drop your plan in the mail or send it via email, give it another read-through, and if necessary, update it. Revise the plan to reflect recent developments (including new personnel), and bring financial information up to the close of the last month or quarter. Avoid printing too many copies at once so you're not tempted to send out an old plan just to get through the stack.

With investors and lenders in particular, your business plan is your calling card. Make sure its presentation puts the best face on your business and helps move your company closer to its goals.

Following Up

Your job is not done once you have sent out your business plan; you'll have to follow up with potential funding sources to make sure you actually receive an answer. Some banks or investors tell you exactly when you can expect to hear from them. Others are far less communicative. Don't be surprised if you have to take the initiative.

You can call or email for the first time about a week after sending your plan to make sure it has been received. You have a better chance of having your message read or listened to if it's not too long. If you've worked on your "elevator pitch" (see pages 26-27), you can quickly explain the nature of your business.

If an intermediary suggested you contact the funding source, use that name right away. In an email message, you might put the intermediary's name in the subject line to entice the recipient to open your message.

When making initial contact with a potential funder, your voicemail message might be something like:

Phil Turner suggested I call you about my new food products and service company, AAA, Inc. Phil thought our approach to growth and our established customer base would interest you. I'd appreciate the chance to speak with you. I can be reached at 650-555-1000 or you can email me at arnie at aaa.com. I will also try you again in a couple of days. Thank you.

Your email message can be similar to your voicemail. You can include your website address if you have one and you're willing to have the potential funder see it before they've talked to you. Refrain from including any attachments, especially in your first contact. Avoid vague subject lines such as "Great Business Opportunity" or "New Business Venture." You don't want your recipient to think your message is spam.

Generally, refrain from contacting any funding source more frequently than every two weeks. And if they ask you not to call, DON'T.

Nine Surefire Ways to
Ruin Your Business Plan

1 ### Make basic mistakes

Leave out key information or get basic facts wrong, and you'll mess up your entire business plan. Do your homework so you're familiar with standard industry practices. Educate yourself about distribution channels, price markups, regulations, and legal and accounting matters. One error can ruin all your projections and assumptions.

2 ### Underestimate the competition

The worst thing you can say in a business plan is "There is no competition." No matter how unique or terrific your product or service, if you don't have competition, it means there's no market for what you're selling. Be sure to consider potential future competition once you've proven the concept.

3 ### Overestimate sales

When you launch a product or service that's better, faster, or cheaper than the competition's, it's natural to assume customers will beat a path to your door. They won't. Be realistic, even conservative, about how difficult it will be to build a customer base and how long it will take.

4 ### Plan more than one business at a time

Even though your business may eventually have a number of revenue streams, concentrate on one part of it at a time. Show you can be successful in one area before branching out.

5 ### Go it alone

Nobody can build a successful business alone. Strategic alliances, particularly with strong existing businesses, can improve your chances of success. And if you want your business to grow, you'll need to attract and keep capable management and personnel. Show you can work well and creatively with others to leverage your resources.

6 ### Use "phantom" numbers

Don't use financial projections just because they sound good. Don't use "boilerplate" numbers: industry averages might not apply in your situation. Be able to substantiate where you got your numbers and why you made your financial assumptions. Always overestimate expenses and underestimate income.

7 Forget a "Sources and Use of Funds" statement

Financing sources want to see exactly how much money you'll need, how you intend to use it, what money you're contributing, and whether you are expecting to get funds from other sources. If you don't include this information in a clear, concise format, you'll confuse potential investors or lenders.

8 Omit an exit plan

While you may plan on running your business forever, others who invest in your company want to know how they'll get their money out. It's usually not enough for them to just get an annual return; they will want a way to make their original investment "liquid."

9 Lie

This is the best way to get a business plan rejected, increase the chances of your business failing, and ruin your reputation. While every business plan is developed with a certain degree of optimism, when the plan becomes fiction, you're in trouble.

The Experts Talk

Wouldn't it be wonderful if you could enter the minds of the people who will read your business plan—if you could learn what kinds of plans they read, what kinds they toss, and exactly what compels them to give a plan a thumbs up or a thumbs down?

Now you can. On the following pages, you'll find interviews with four people who read business plans for a living: two angel investors, a venture capitalist, and a bank loan professional.

They'll tell you in their own words:

- What kinds of information different financing professionals look for in a plan.

- What sections they turn to first.

- What they want to know about your team, your business, and your market.

- What aspects of a plan's presentation they like—and dislike.

- What could destroy your chances of getting financing or meeting your other objectives.

Some of the experts take you beyond the plan review, explaining what happens *after* a plan is accepted. They provide valuable information on the kind of involvement they seek in the companies they finance— as well as how the ongoing professional relationship between the entrepreneur and the financing individuals or institution really works.

Before you take your plan to your readers, learn from the experienced experts interviewed here. Their ideas will help you create a winning plan, determine exactly who should read it, and significantly boost its chances for success.

Tony Shipley, Angel Investor

Tony Shipley is Chairman of Queen City Angels, a Cincinnati-based group of investors focused on technology companies. He also serves as Chairman of CH Mack, a Cincinnati information technology company. He has extensive experience in entrepreneurial companies, having served as the CEO of a startup that was later selected for the Inc. 500 list. He is a member of various business organizations and serves on several boards. Shipley has also won numerous awards for entrepreneurship and business achievement.

In general, what type of information do you, as an angel investor, look for in a business plan?

The first thing we want to know is: Does the product or service solve a specific customer problem, and what is that problem? Essentially, what is the *value proposition*? Then we'd also want to know who in the customer's organization *owns* that problem. In other words, who is the prospective target customer for the company?

Another thing we're interested in is management. When you're writing the check to fund an organization, at the end of the day, you're betting on the people. You need a strong belief that the management has the wherewithal to run the enterprise and execute the plan. Companies seeking early seed-type of investments, however, often have incomplete management teams. That's OK; we don't expect them to be a fully developed team at that point, but we expect the startups to recognize their limitations, to see the gaps in the team, and have a plan for filling them.

Also, when we invest, we've got to have a fairly clear vision of what the exit strategy looks like. We want to be able to get our money out in four to five years at the low end and in seven to eight years at the upper end.

What do you consider red flags or deal breakers in a plan?

A major problem is a proposed funding plan we feel is inadequate to allow the company to achieve certain milestones we believe are important to attract a follow-up round of investment.

Sometimes, entrepreneurs don't identify the person or group they're talking to in a customer's organization [their target customer]. That raises issues when it comes to evaluating their sales model.

A third problem occurs when the CEO or other executives are not "coachable." We learned a long time ago that no one knows everything, and we recognize the value in that. We like it when teams see their weaknesses and are willing to take input via our mentoring activities.

What type of business plan format do you prefer?

We ask that companies initially submit a five-page executive summary and an application. Staff members initially review the summaries to make sure they have the essential format elements, then distribute them to the angel investors. This gives the angels a snapshot of the business model, and if that snapshot is compelling enough, we ask for the full business plan.

How long should the final business plan be?

We don't expect a dissertation. We find that the smarter people are, the more articulate they are and the more concisely they can write. In general, the main body of the plan usually runs about 10 to 20 pages, but the appendices can make the plan quite thick.

What is the range of money you invest?

In our angel group, we're looking at the low end of $200,000 to $300,000 and the upper end of $1 million to $2 million.

What types of businesses do you fund?

We try to fund businesses in and around the Cincinnati area. As angel investors, we want to be close enough to jump in the car and drive to their site when they've got a crisis. We have found that most angel groups don't venture too far outside of their geographical area.

We tend to focus on technology companies and medical companies that have a tech orientation, like medical device companies.

How long does the whole process take, from the time the entrepreneur submits the plan to the time they get an answer?

With nominal due diligence [research], the whole process could last from three to six weeks. If we have to do in-depth due diligence, it could be several months.

What kind of role in the company do you expect when making an investment?

Our involvement varies, but we're not just about writing checks and walking away. Many of these companies are really in need of mentoring at this stage. At a minimum, we want to take board seats, but we also like to have people (angels) take advisory seats and offer consulting services. We feel it's important to provide hands-on involvement, to help entrepreneurs get over the hurdles that every new business must overcome. For us, stepping in and providing expertise is part of the fun. If we were just about writing checks, there are a thousand other ways for us to make money.

Albert Martinez, Banker

Located in the startup capital of the world, Silicon Valley Bank (SVB) is a different kind of financial institution. SVB has, for more than 35 years, helped finance and support startups and entrepreneurs, as well as provide banking services to global companies. Albert Martinez leads SVB's relationship management team and has been with SVB for over 25 years.

What geographic area do you serve and what range of money do you lend?

Historically, we serve all of Northern California, but Silicon Valley Bank is global. We have offices throughout the U.S. and in India, China, Israel, and the U.K. and can make funding decisions worldwide. The majority of our deals are one to five million dollars. But we do as little as $250,000.

In general, what type of information do you look for, as a banker, in a business plan?

The first thing we look for is clarity. Clarity goes hand in hand with brevity. We look for a really good opportunity and that the entrepreneur has a good idea of where they're going. You can usually see it in the first couple of paragraphs or slides. You look for focus. Technology can be applied in so many different ways, and if a company talks about all the different ways it could go, then that lack of focus can lead it to become distracted over time. We look for a business plan that clearly states: Here's what we have, here's the market we're going after, here's the scope or size of that market. The plan needs to be very specific as opposed to something nebulous, with multiple markets and multiple technologies.

Many entrepreneurs think that flexibility is a selling point, so they go after everything. But to be successful, they must focus on a particular path rather than saying that this technology can be applied to all these different verticals and do all these different things.

How much time do you spend assessing a business plan?

When we're evaluating a company, we spend a fair amount of time with the business plan itself. We'll spend an hour or two with the company, have follow-up meetings with its investors, and then spend more time digesting the information and writing up an evaluation.

What do you consider the most important aspects of the plan?

The most important pieces are the problem being solved and the statement of that problem. We look at how clear that statement is. There must be a basic understanding of the need for their business. After that, we look for an explanation of the market: the market size and who the other players are. They must have a clear understanding of what they need to accomplish to be successful. That may change over time, but they need to have a plan.

In what order would you like the various sections of the plan to appear? What part do you read first?

The entrepreneur needs to start out with the most compelling attribute they have; perhaps it's the technology itself, but very often it's the team and the history. Right at the beginning, they need to show us why we'd be interested in the company. What differentiates them from others should come out in the first couple of paragraphs. It can be the past success of a couple team members—who they are and their expertise.

If it's a tech company entering an area in which others have failed because of the technology, we want to see a brief description of the technology and why others couldn't accomplish what this company will accomplish. We want to understand how this company is different.

What do you want to know about the competition?

We're definitely focused on the competition. To the extent that it's direct competition, that part of the plan should go into detail. If your direct competition is cheaper, faster, and better, we have to understand how you'll succeed.

What do you consider red flags?

Many of the companies we work with are already funded [by venture capitalists or others], so many red flags have been addressed. One red flag is a lack of clarity. Some entrepreneurs will use a lot of words but not really say anything, and that's a red flag. We want to see that someone can succinctly explain their business, that they understand the market, and that they can explain everything in layman's terms. If they're not clear on what they're trying to accomplish, that's a red flag.

What else is a red flag? When they say there is no competition. They need to be thoughtful and informative in how they discuss their competition.

And we like to see a reasonable amount of awareness of risk. Being honest about what the risks are and how they will mitigate those risks is important. You don't have to have all the answers, but identifying those risk factors is valuable. If we end up identifying risks that the company is unaware of, that's not a positive thing.

What do you look for when judging the potential return on investment?

As a lender, from a debt perspective, we want all these companies to turn on monetization at some point. We want to see that if they take an investment, they will use it to create value. With technology, for example, if they have enough users, they will generate revenue, and if they create enough value, they will repay the debt. There may be strong user growth and engagement that may have staying power and create value. Instagram, for instance, had no equity, but it had created value.

Lauren Flanagan, Angel Investor

Lauren Flanagan is cofounder and Managing Director of BELLE Capital USA (www.bellevc. com), an early stage angel investment fund, located in the greater Chicago area. Belle invests solely in companies with women in leadership positions. Flanagan has more than 25 years experience founding and operating technology companies, and she was the founder of four technology companies. She is also cofounder and managing director of the Phenomenelle Angels Fund. Businessweek once named her one of the top 25 angels in technology. She is Executive Chairman of the Current Motor Company.

What type of businesses does Belle Capital fund?

We invest in women-led companies that are scalable to $20 million or more. They have to be capital efficient and have significant intellectual property, so they tend to be technology or technology-related companies. For Belle Capital, we're looking for at least one woman in the "C" suite of officers [CEO, COO, CFO, CMO] or a commitment to putting women in the C suite and on the board.

How many business plans do you review a year?

We receive hundreds of business plans a month. We don't read them all. We have an automated application process on our website [www.bellevc.com, VC Pitch]. If we're interested, we ask for a business plan. We can tell in a matter of minutes if it's a business we're interested in.

What do you look for in a company that you're considering investing in?

We ask, "What is the market problem?"

Is the solution a "must-have" rather than a "nice-to-have"? Can it be made a "must-have"? Once people know about it, will they feel they absolutely have to have it? And what is the urgency of the problem?

We look at their "go-to-market" plan that lets their potential customers know they exist. If people don't know you exist, you're not going to scale very easily. We look at their competitors. If they say "There is no competition," there's no market, or they just don't understand the competition.

We're also looking for superior management: a team, not just a sole proprietor. We like to see that at least one has been an entrepreneur. If they've only worked with corporations, they don't know what startup life is like, and they're not prepared. We're investing in a group of people, and we look at their ability to work together. At least one should have started a business before. Even if it failed, there can be a lot of learning from that.

What specific considerations do you have as an angel investor?

We need a company that is scalable and capital efficient. As an angel investor group, we're not in a position to fund businesses that need $25 million—lots of capital—like venture capitalists. We want to understand how we're going to make money; after all, we're investors.

Angels want to have liquidity within five years, seven years max. We look for companies in which we can make money in a three-to-five year window. Things that take a lot of time and a lot of money aren't appropriate for angels, such as finding new drugs or new energy sources. That's why you see a lot of angels in tech and tech services; they're not as capital intensive, and they can be liquid in a shorter period. But even in life sciences and energy, there are capital-efficient companies.

What are some of the most important aspects of the business plan?

The classic elevator pitch is very important to us. If an entrepreneur can't describe their concept quickly, it's hard to syndicate the deal—to raise money from others. Angels typically co-invest with other angels. We have to talk to others about the opportunity, and we have to be able to explain it in a clear and simple way.

What's a common mistake that entrepreneurs make in their business plan?

People don't sell themselves and their team enough, especially women. One entrepreneur neglected to say she was an astronaut! Women feel they should be modest and not brag. If you've done anything amazing, you should lead with it. It can be something remarkable outside of business: you've been a great athlete, have an amazing skill. I want to hear about success. I want to see evidence that you'll dig in, that you're good at adapting—those are character traits I'm looking for. Also, do a really good job at explaining the team and how they work together. The team really matters to angel investors.

Do any aspects of business plan presentation make a difference?

I really like to see the plan start out with the things that matter. Increasingly, we're seeing people delivering PowerPoints, but they still have to have the essential information of the business plan. We have to see the financials, of course. Having a business plan that is clear and that everyone understands is a sign of a sophisticated management team. If it looks like someone merely did one of those "fill in the blank" business plans, that's just lame.

What do you consider red flags?

No competition is a big red flag. Showing a huge amount of sales in a short period of time, without appropriate staffing levels to achieve that, is another. That means they're wildly unrealistic.

What are some deal breakers for angels?

If it's a "lifestyle" business—the entrepreneur is overly focused on control, never wants to sell—that's a deal breaker. They need an exit.

Philip Schlein, Venture Capitalist

Philip Schlein joined U.S. Venture Partners in Menlo Park, California in 1985 after a successful 28-year career as an operating executive in the retailing industry. For 11 years prior to joining USVP, Schlein was President and CEO of Macy's California. Under his leadership, sales grew from just under $200 million to almost $1.2 billion; profits grew from $17 million to $108 million. He also served on the Board of Directors of Apple Computer for eight years.

While with USVP, Schlein originated a number of investments in the consumer/retail sector including PetSmart, Fresh Choice, and House of Blues. He has also served on the Boards of Directors of iVillage, HomeGrocer.com, and NBCi, among others. He holds a B.S. in Economics from the University of Pennsylvania.

What type of information do you, as a venture capitalist, look for in a business plan?

The first characteristic we look for in a company is the quality of the management team. In all cases, it's important to have the references and to feel good about the people on the team. That's really significant. You could have a good, but not great idea, and a good management team will do what it takes to make it successful.

Then we look at the product. We ask: Is it something that's needed, or just nice to have? Needed means it's going to be really valuable; nice to have is not as valuable. If the product is a "need-to-have," and changes or enhances the way something is done, that indicates there will be a strong market for it.

Of course, the company has to have a business model that makes sense. How are you going to earn income? What are the revenue sources? We generally look at a five-year projection—we expect the first two or three

years to make more sense, the last two or three to be a little more guesswork.

Market size and competition are the next important factors that must be considered.

Finally, we look at how much money is needed to take the business to a point where there could be an IPO or an acquisition. We look at the exit strategy and exit value. But that's only after we've looked at the other things first.

When you receive a plan, in what order do you read the various sections?

I might start by skipping back to see who the management team is. But I certainly want the executive summary up front to see what the company is all about and whether the business model makes sense. If they have patents or have applied for them, that also should be in the executive summary.

I want to see that there's a big enough market and how they differentiate themselves from their competition. Then I look at the financials to see if that validates the business model. They might have a summary financial in the executive summary, but the more detailed information is usually further back.

What do you want to know about the competition?

I want to know how the company is different from what's already out there, and what makes their product a "need-to-have." With technology, you have intellectual property that's protected. That's not the case with consumer businesses, which is why you really need an innovative idea and have to be able to execute it quickly.

What do you want to know about the market?

The size of the market is important. One could develop a great medical device for which there really isn't much need. When you look at the market, it may be so small, it's really not worth investing in.

What do you consider red flags?

Some things that would throw a business plan off are:

- A too-small market size

- Management that has no experience or involvement in a like business area

- A business or product that's not really needed

Sometimes the business model makes no sense, like when someone expects to go from zero to $100 million in two years. Some plans are just off-the-wall.

Do you get many plans that are "off-the-wall"?

The networking in the technology world is pretty tight knit. Usually the people sent to us are referrals, so we don't get as many off-the-wall plans there. It's different in the consumer world, though. I get plans that are off-the-wall, over-the-counter, onto-the-door, through-the-woods, and every other way. Sometimes, I don't even know the people they say referred them to me. I get a whole mixture.

What are some deal breakers? What will make you immediately decide to reject a plan?

It could be an unrealistic valuation* on the company. When we look at the exit value, it just doesn't make sense for us. Or the market might be too small for us. In that case, we might find smaller VC firms to help them. Sometimes, the plan just falls outside of what our core expertise and investment strategy are at any given time.

Valuation is the value of a company's stock based on its earnings and the market value of its assets.

What is the range of money you invest?

It really depends on the business, but $8-10 million is the minimum we would invest. We could have as much as $20 million in a business. We also invest in several rounds. For example, we might only have $1 million invested in a seed stage of financing.

What kinds of businesses most interest you?

We do life sciences, especially medical devices. We do semiconductors, telecommunications, software, enterprise technology. We don't do too much with companies selling direct to the consumer these days.

What size of companies do you finance, and at what stage do you come in?

For medical devices, we could come in reasonably early. With technology companies, it could be very early, maybe just at the point where they have the intellectual property. If it's a consumer business, we'd come in at a later stage, perhaps after they've opened two or three stores and some of the risk has been taken out of it. In many cases, we'd want the company to have at least one or two customers.

Do you prefer that a company's financing come mainly from you or from many different sources?

Most of the time, we have a VC partner. We might do something alone where we give some startup money to a very early stage company. Generally, we bring in partners, or they bring us in; it works both ways.

What do you notice first about a plan's physical presentation?

If it's too fancy, I get nervous, as I do when I walk into offices that are really fancy. I'd be wondering how they're spending their money. If a plan looked like a design firm put it together, I'd get nervous, unless it

came from a very aesthetic business, which we usually don't invest in anyway.

What is a good length for a business plan?

The fewest number of pages needed to get the message across. If you think about it, you really don't need a lot. You can do an appendix with information that you don't necessarily have to include in the basic plan.

We get plans of all sizes. Sometimes, people go on and on, and are redundant, giving us 50 or 60 pages when it can be done in 30. You begin to wonder if that person is focused, and focus is really important in the success of a company.

How much and what kind of supporting data should be included (such as studies, surveys, graphs, and charts)?

Again, it depends on the business. Pictures only help if they explain something or show how something works. Sometimes medical people have pictures to show how a device would work or how it would enter the body. In the consumer world, they could present pictures of the product line they're dealing with. Generally, though, it's what they say that matters.

How much time do you spend reading a plan?

It depends on the plan and what time of night it is. (I generally don't read anything in the office.) And it depends on how interesting it is, how pertinent it is; it's just like reading a book. In general, I just plow through all of them.

What type of involvement do you look for in the companies you finance?

In almost all of the cases, the businesses are fairly early stage, and we're on the board. But there are a few cases where a company is already more established and we aren't board members. We decide to invest anyway because we think the size is going to be good, and there are already other venture groups involved.

"I want to know how the company is different from what's already out there, and what makes their product a 'need-to-have.'"

—Philip Schlein, Venture Capitalist

Enzo Torresi, Angel Investor

Enzo Torresi is the founder of EuroFund, a Silicon Valley–based firm that invests in seed and early stage financing of software, communications, Internet, and wireless technology startups. He is also a partner in myQube, a high-tech venture fund based in Milan. Torresi has more than 35 years experience in the computer industry and has founded six companies.

What kinds of companies interest angel investors (as opposed to venture capitalists and other investors)?

Angels tend to look at very early stage companies where there's much higher risk. We provide the real seed financing. VCs nowadays go for the first or second round of financing, after the initial proof-of-concept stage. The first year of money is usually from the angels.

I finance companies that don't even have an office address yet. They have a concept, and they're shopping for money to get them off the ground. The only things that count at that stage are the idea, the founder, and the CEO.

What types of companies do you look for?

I mainly finance tech companies, those with intellectual property [such as patentable technology]. I don't do idea companies. The companies I most often fund are very small—the whole staff might consist of the CEO and CTO.

What is the range of money you invest?

Our investment is typically in the range of $50K to 100K. If you ask the other angels in Silicon Valley, they'd say $25K to 100K.

Do you prefer to be the sole initial investor in a company, or do you like to see financing from other sources?

I never do it myself. I like to have company—two or three other investors. Typically, when I decide to invest, I call some friends I've invested with before and tell them, "I saw something interesting. It's a good idea; send a check." They do the same with me.

What type of information most interests you in a business plan?

The founder's experience is very important. The only thing you can base your decision on is their track record, and how they make the presentation.

What kind of founder track record do you look for?

Everyone has different expectations, but I look at how many "bounces" they've had. If someone has had five employers in 10 years, that's a warning signal to me. They usually say they're creative, or they've had bad bosses. I know someone can be trapped in a big corporate scenario with the wrong boss and decide to do something different after a few years, but if it becomes a pattern, I tend to think it's a problem with them.

Lack of references is another problem. I've personally used the strategy of never burning bridges, which has helped me a lot. I'm skeptical of people who have lost contact with, alienated, or hate their previous bosses. I think it's a bad sign. If you can be a team player in a big company, that's a prerequisite to being a good manager. If you cannot be a team player, what's to say you can lead a team?

What do you consider the most important aspects of a business plan?

In general, the plan has to show the idea, the execution plan, and an analysis of the competition.

The most important part of the plan is the idea or description—the concept. It should not just show the knowledge or execution of the idea, but also what we call the *secret sauce*: What has this founder figured out that others have not?

You also want to know if there's a market, and if the idea can actually be executed. Somebody might say: "I have the idea of

going to Saturn." Sure, there's a market, but it can't happen. There are a lot of naïve ideas that sound like this; they can't be done and are a waste of time. You'd be surprised how many entrepreneurs get defensive about that.

What do you want to know about the competition?

I want to know all *they* know about it. In many cases, I'll know more about a competitor than they do.

If someone tells me, "I have no competition," I get upset. I want to know why they think that. That's how I learn what the person understands about marketing, competition, and their customers. If I catch them underestimating, undermentioning, or not mentioning an obvious competitor, that's a big red flag. Some of them know they have competition; they just hate to admit it. Even worse are those who don't even know they have it.

In what order do you read the various sections of the business plan?

Well, everyone seems to follow some sort of template, but I first go to the management team section. The next thing I look at is the financial plan.

There's usually an opening statement. That's very important. Usually it's in the cover letter or somewhere at the beginning of the plan. If a company or a founder cannot articulate in a paragraph what they are doing, that's trouble. If they have to go into a convoluted five-page description of it, they're going to have problems explaining it to their salespeople and their sales partners. I think that's very common.

You mentioned three potential red flags: a questionable founder track record, a lack of a competitive analysis, and a convoluted concept description. What are some others?

Another one is a lack of a financial forecast. Often, entrepreneurs don't do one because they think it's too early. They say, "I don't know if I'm going to get the money, so I can't do a financial plan." I tell them, "You're also judged on how you make your assumptions."

An assumption could be: I'm going to raise a million dollars in VC financing; I'm going to hire a VP of marketing and a sales manager. Some entrepreneurs are afraid of getting nailed by the investors, of someone saying, "You're going to spend *this* much in a year?" But most angels and VCs know there have got to be some assumptions behind the plan. If you can't develop a financial plan until you get financing, that's a real problem, because everyone wants to know how you plan to spend the money.

What happens, then, if the assumptions, the idea, or the execution of the idea laid out in the plan change over time?

At the beginning, no company adheres exactly to the initial business plan. Many times, I've seen a complete reversal of the idea after giving someone money. It's not really a problem. I always say, if it's a smart team, they'll figure it out. They know the general direction in which they're going.

It's much more of a problem if a company sticks to a particular course in spite of evidence that it's not going to work. Sometimes we call that *founderitis*, when founders are so consumed by an idea and won't change their minds.

I generally see the plan as a zigzag. You've just got to find the right *zig*. That's why, in the initial interview, I look for people who are flexible, to the point of admitting they might have the wrong *zig*.

Do you look for certain keywords or buzzwords in a plan?

Generally, buzzwords are a turnoff, especially if it's clear the entrepreneur doesn't really understand the area. Buzzwords can actually raise a red flag; they open you up to more questioning. If you don't fully understand the concept, you can get nailed by the angel or VC reading a plan.

Never underestimate the knowledge of [the investors in] your audience. Chances are, once you go to present your plan, someone in the room is going to be an expert in the area you're talking about. If a CEO or CTO gives a presentation, and it's clear they don't understand the technology, that's instant death. I've never seen anyone recover from that.

What's an acceptable length for the business plan?

I prefer plans that are 10 to 15 pages; maybe 20 pages maximum. I don't know anyone who will read a 30-page plan.

What kind of format do you prefer?

I like to see lots of graphics, like flow charts showing the architecture of a new technology. I don't like big blocks of text, but I don't like too many bullets either, unless they truly represent a concise way of looking at the concept.

Some business plans are really very badly written; they use long words, and long convoluted statements. A lot of people have a hard time putting their ideas down in 10 pages, but to me, that's a test of how concise their thinking can be. I value conciseness.

What are your preferences regarding submission of the plan? Do you prefer mail? Fax? Email?

I get a lot of plans over email. There's nothing I can do about it; people find out you're an angel or VC and start sending you their plans. I'm developing a theory that if I receive it by FedEx, it has a better chance. So I guess the hierarchy in terms of my preference would be: 1) FedEx; 2) regular mail; 3) fax; 4) email. Email has made the unsolicited stuff much easier to broadcast for the creator, but it ends up in one big basket with all the Viagra ads and other spam. A good honest business plan could easily get lost in there.

How long do you spend looking at a business plan?

Well, on these unidentified flying objects as I call them [unsolicited email plans], I spend very little time; I really just look at the cover letter. If it doesn't say in the body of the e-mail what they are doing, I don't even download the attachment. To me, it's very rude to send an attachment without saying what it is. If I do end up looking at the plan, I'll probably spend about five or 10 minutes on it. I'll look at the concept, and see if I recognize any of the founders. If it's something that interests me, I'll usually give them a call right away.

So then how long does the entire process take, from the time you receive the plan to the time you make your decision?

With me, it can be as short as a couple of days. If the plan interests me, they'll come in for a presentation. It either happens at the presentation or it doesn't. In that 45 minutes to an hour, you've got to make up your mind whether you trust your money to that person. That's really the bottom line. That's where I make my decision.

"It's much more of a problem if a company sticks to a particular course in spite of evidence that it's not going to work. Sometimes we call that founderitis, when founders are so consumed by an idea and won't change their minds."

—Enzo Torresi, Angel Investor

Business Planning During a Recession. Now What?!

Covid-19 presented exceptional challenges to all businesses, especially small businesses. But can challenging times lead to successful companies?

While a recession may seem like a tough time to launch, run, or grow a business, history has shown us that challenging economic conditions also create opportunities. Many successful businesses that are now household names actually started in recessions, the Great Depression, or in other down markets: General Electric, IBM, General Motors, Disney, Burger King, Microsoft, CNN, Apple, WhatsApp, Venmo, Groupon, Uber, Square, Hewlett-Packard, Hyatt, Trader Joe's, FedEx, Electronic Arts, Airbnb, and many more.

In fact, a 2009 Kauffman Foundation study found that more than half the companies in the Fortune 500 were started during recessions or bear markets.

Why? How can a bad economy be a good time to start or grow a business?

- Customers are more open to change.

- Customers seek new, often less expensive, ways to meet their needs.

- Customers have new needs.

- Competitors may have higher fixed costs than you do.

- Competitors reduce their marketing.

- Competitors are weakened or discouraged.

In an economic downturn, a smart, nimble, hardworking competitor often has a leg up on even large, well-established big companies. You can go after their customers, devise new products or services to meet their changing needs, or look for weakened or disheartened competitors to acquire.

And it's not just that a down economy presents new opportunities; starting a business during recessionary times actually provides a few advantages over starting in high growth times such as lower costs on critical business needs, more ability to negotiate with vendors, and more available talent to hire.

Take heart:
The economy will change

Whatever situation you are in, sooner or later, it's going to change. The economic situation goes through cycles. History proves that the American economy—like the Canadian, European, and much of the rest of the world's economies—is resilient.

You can be resilient too. Keep in mind:

- If you have products or services people wanted and needed before the recession, they'll continue to want and need them.

- You have it in you to forge your own destiny.

- Down economies present opportunities as well as challenges.

- You'll have to work hard, make changes, and face failures. But you have it in you to do all those things. As an entrepreneur, you knew there would be risk. You're not faint at heart.

Of course, you'll need to make some changes to your business plan. But in a recession, one of your greatest strategic advantages may be your willingness to work hard, work smart, and keep at it, while others often will not.

Existing businesses: Think of yourself as a startup

Given the new reality—that you have to be nimble, change to meet new conditions, seize opportunities, work harder and longer—it's helpful to think of yourself as a startup even if you've been in business for years. In a reces-sion—in a vastly changing economy and society—no matter how long you've been in business, you are actually starting fresh, anew.

For existing businesses, it may be challeng-ing to think of yourself as a startup since you've been at this for a while—but it's a good way to approach running your com-pany right now. Of course, you probably have some baggage that real startups don't have: leases, bills, inventory, employees, and more. But you also have a wealth of resources startups don't have: loyal custom-ers, vendor relations, experienced employ-ees, industry knowledge, and contacts.

Embracing the idea of being a startup gives you more energy and a more positive out-look. You'll learn new ways of doing busi-ness, new things about your customers and potential customers, new ways that your industry is improving, new ways to manage money and manage people.

Stay agile, move fast

Businesses that survive are businesses that can change. As with your body, if you just sit in the same position, you get stiff and old. If you want to survive the current situation and thrive for the long-term, you've got to stay flexible in terms of your own attitude.

Minimal viable product

As you think like a startup, embrace the concept of "MVP," or minimal viable product. Basically, a minimal viable product is a product or service that has been created quickly, meeting only the absolutely necessary level of quality to meet customers' basic needs, in order to get it to market as soon as possible. Over time, and seeing the experience of actual customers, the product is improved and refined and revised.

That's right—attitude. The single most important thing in preparing your business to survive in challenging economic times is your attitude. That may sound a bit simplistic, but it's true. And while a positive, flexible attitude certainly does not guarantee success in recessionary times, a negative, do-nothing attitude almost certainly guarantees failure.

In good times, you can often avoid changing. After all, things are rolling along smoothly. The beginning of succeeding in a recession is to recognize you will have to change, you will sometimes fail, and you will often be discouraged. But your own belief in yourself and your ability to tackle new situations will help you survive and succeed.

Be willing and able to "pivot"

"Pivot" is a word you'll hear frequently in a challenging economy. You might be in—or plan—one type of business but find yourself needing to change—to pivot—to another. Why?

- What you're doing is not working—it's time for "Plan B" and then "Plan C."

- The changing business landscape presents opportunities you want to seize.

- One part of your business takes off, and you want to lean in to that growth.

- Your market is rapidly changing.

- Your industry is rapidly changing, particularly due to technological change.

- Economic, health, regulatory, or other external issues force you to change.

- Something better comes along.

And, of course, we saw how Covid-19 caused a massive need for change in how most businesses do business. A changing world creates new needs, and needs create opportunities.

For example, when the pandemic caused the closure of many restaurants, some pivoted to begin providing takeout, even if they'd never offered it before. That was a first, and relatively easy, step for most. But some restaurant owners found additional sources of new revenue, by selling meal kits and grocery items or conducting online cooking classes.

Some went even further. For example, a small chain of shops selling handcrafted ice cream in Seattle was suddenly closed at the beginning of the pandemic. The owner laid off virtually her entire staff and things looked bleak. But she pivoted—she started packaging and selling her ice cream to grocery stores. In doing so, she added a new line of business for her company—one that lasted after she was able to reopen her stores. That pivot helped her not only survive in the short run, but grow substantially.

If you are just launching a business, there's a good chance that you have to veer away from your original concept, change your business model, even dramatically change the kinds of goods or services you thought you were going to offer. Even if you're new, you may find you have to "pivot."

Start lean, stay lean

In a nutshell: Staying "lean" means spending/buying/owning the least amount you need to run—and grow—your business.

188 | BUSINESS PLAN IN A DAY

Being lean not only means you keep more of your money—it means you are less bogged down by the infrastructure and cost of your operations.

For example—a food truck is "leaner" than a brick-and-mortar restaurant. The food truck can literally move to find different customers, can easily change the type of food offered, has fewer employees, and has a vehicle lease instead of a long lease on a building. A catering service might be even leaner than a food truck if the owner uses a commercial kitchen only when they have a gig.

Keep fixed costs down

Not all expenses are alike. First, you have "fixed" expenses that you have to pay every month (or week or year) regardless of how much you sell, such as rent, payment on term loans, equipment and vehicle leases, insurance.

The inflexibility of fixed expenses—your overhead or "nut"—makes responding to changing conditions more challenging. Fixed expenses are the ones that keep you up at night and can actually cause you to shutter your business entirely. So, you need to do everything you can to reduce or eliminate fixed expenses.

Rent

This is the killer. What can you do to reduce your rent?

- **If you do have to enter into a lease, negotiate hard.** Try to make the lease as short as possible, have provisions allowing you to sublease, and—if at all possible—do not sign a lease where you have to give a personal guarantee.

- **Don't rent anything unless you have to.** Obviously, if you're starting a brick-and-mortar store or restaurant, you need space. But if you are in services, technology, or construction, for example, see if you can find other spaces to work from.

- **Use "rent-as-you-go" space.** Look for shared workspaces, rental kitchens, or local businesses that may have extra space to rent out short-term.

- **Work from home.** When you start a business, initially you may have to work from home and work remotely with others on your team.

- **Renegotiate your lease.** If you already have a lease, see if you can lower it. Commercial real estate typically faces a vacancy crisis as a result of an economic downturn. Most property owners can't afford to lose existing tenants. Try to work with them to lower your rent, delay payments, and shorten the lease length.

Term loans and equipment/vehicle leases

Loans may represent the other big headache for you. So be sure to examine and negotiate hard on any fixed long-term obligations.

Interest rates are, at the time of this writing, at a very low rate. So, if you already have such commitments, the first thing to do is to negotiate with your vendors on lowering your interest rate or allowing you to forgo a number of current payments—tacking them on to the end of the term—to help you weather a downturn.

Another option is to look for other sources with lower interest rates—such as a new loan, line-of-credit, or SBA/other government financing program—that would enable you to pay off this fixed expense now and replace it with a lower cost option.

Expenses that look fixed but really aren't

Many of your regular monthly bills are always the same amount. But there's probably some room for you to lower those costs. For instance, you will probably use a number of cloud-based services; you may be able to reduce the level of service or number of seats you pay for. Or you may have insurance that provides a certain level of coverage or add-on coverages that you may be able to reduce.

Be careful before you commit to any fixed expenses and set aside some time to look at all your current fixed expenses to see how you can reduce some of those costs.

Reduce variable expenses

Variable expenses—inventory, raw materials, staff—sound easy to reduce, since they change depending on how much demand there is for your products or services. But how variable are they? After all, you need inventory to be able to entice and sell to your customers. You need staff to be able to provide your services. You need raw materials to manufacture your products. That means making decisions about purchasing before you actually make a sale.

In general, when dealing with variable expenses, keep the following in mind:

- **Choose vendors based on more than price.** Look for their ability to fill orders fast, give you generous payment terms, their reliability, and the ability for you to pay with credit cards if you need to.

- **Purchase carefully.** Examine past sales records if you're an existing business, do your research, and forecast sales conservatively. It may be better to lose a sale than to spend too much on inventory, raw materials, or supplies.

- **Look at all recurring expenses.** Research what competitors charge, ask for a deal, negotiate, and be willing to switch.

Reduce inventory

Never forget this phrase: "Inventory is money sitting around in a different form."

You can't spend money that's tied up in inventory on experimenting with new business lines, marketing or hiring a new salesperson, or paying your rent or health insurance.

When planning your business, build in practices that keep your inventory levels always as low as possible. But if you're already in business with inventory sitting around, the following offers can turn that inventory into ready cash:

- Multiple purchase or bulk purchase discounts

- Bundled products or services with a large discount

- Deals such as "Special of the Day"

- Extremely steep discounts

- Gifts to referral sources

- Gifts to good customers

- Donations of gifts in kind for marketing purposes as a last resort

Learn to love "just-in-time"

With a "just-in-time" inventory management system, you get the inventory you need just when you need it and reduce the amount you have to pay before your customers pay you.

In book publishing, for example, print on demand (POD) has been rapidly growing. Fast, efficient book-printing machines can quickly print a "one-off" book—one that's out of print or not in great demand—just when a customer orders a copy.

Of course, just-in-time has its downsides, including higher costs, the risk that supplies don't arrive in time, or the rush order is of lower quality. To reduce risk, seek out vendors with quick turnaround times that are geographically close (for faster shipping), and develop a good relationship with

them. You'll also need an efficient flow of information from sales teams to purchasing teams. Encouraging customers to preorder—and prepay—will also significantly reduce the inventory you need on hand.

Have your vendors "own" your inventory

The absolute best just-in-time scenario is one in which you never actually own anything you sell until you actually sell it. Ideally, you don't ever touch the product or service.

Jeff Bezos started the "largest bookstore in the world" without ever owning a book or shipping a book. He knew that the bookselling industry had distributors and wholesalers who stocked huge inventories of books, which they could send to customers directly when Amazon placed an order. Bezos was able to spend his money on building his online "bookstore" without having to spend his funds on actual books.

The name for this very attractive arrangement is "dropshipping" and you don't need a web storefront to do it. Whatever your line of business, search for suppliers, distributors, or wholesalers who will do direct fulfillment of their inventory and bill you as products are shipped. If you run an ecommerce store

Diversify your supply chain

The companies you rely on—your supply chain—to provide you with incoming goods are essential to your business operations. During a downturn, you will likely experience some difficulties and delays with your suppliers at some point. They may be short of stock, have lengthy delivery times, or get out of the business altogether. Try not to be dependent on just one supplier; your financial future will be too vulnerable if it fails you.

on Shopify, it works with a service called Oberlo (www.Oberlo.com) to help you find dropship goods and suppliers.

Outsource everything you can

Stay lean in your business with "just-in-time" everything: staff, business services, equipment, vehicles, delivery, whatever. If you can hire just what you need, when you need it, for only as long as you need it, you'll keep money in your bank account.

Do this by outsourcing as many aspects of your business to others as you can. Of course, you may pay more for each hour, service, or product than if you had in-house staff, your own manufacturing, or equipment and vehicles you own, but you have much more flexibility and far less initial outlay. In fact, you can grow a fairly big—and profitable—company by letting others do most of the work for you.

For example, many companies outsource:

- The manufacturing of their products

- Their technical support services

- The sales and distribution of their products

- Their janitorial services

By outsourcing, you can introduce a new product or service without investing in the infrastructure of creating it in-house.

Expand how you think about making sales

During a booming economy, a business might not need to think about different ways to make sales. During a down economy, you may have to get more creative. Consider some of the many ways you can make sales, including:

- **Direct sales.** An end-use customer buys directly from you without any intermediary.

- **Ecommerce.** Customers buy from your website.

- **Platform sales.** Customers buy your products online from another website.

Outsource employees, but control your data

When setting up and managing cloud-based applications:

- Ensure you are always the administrator/owner of every cloud-based application.

- You must have access to all data of every employee.

- Set up administrative controls that let you bypass private passwords.

- When an employee leaves, turn off their access to your cloud-based applications immediately (if you are firing or laying them off, do so before you tell them). You control the application and data, not the departing employee (and they can't hold your data hostage).

- **Wholesale.** Customers who plan to re-sell your products buy them from you at large discounts.

- **Distributor.** Another company sells your products to others and takes a percentage of the sale or a fee.

- **Social media sales.** You sell from your social media presence.

- **Subscription sales.** A customer pays an ongoing fee to get your products or services on a regular basis.

- **Membership.** A customer pays a fee to join and receive certain perks, such as discounts or special treatment.

- **Licensing.** You are paid to allow your name to be used by another company on its products or services.

- **White labeling.** You make a product or service that others market under their own brand.

Enable ecommerce on your website

Customers like the convenience and safety of buying things directly from the web. As you plan your business, have ecommerce in mind, even if you don't feel you have a product or service that lends itself to being purchased online.

A number of platforms make it easy to add shopping capabilities to a business' online presence, such as:

- Shopify (www.shopify.com)

- SquareSpace (www.squarespace.com)

- Wix (www.wix.com)

- WordPress (www.wordpress.org)

Some of these have built-in gift card options, which enable virtually any business-to-consumer company to make online sales.

Choose a niche

It's often far easier for a small or startup company to attract customers by focusing on a specific market segment—or niche—rather than trying to win every customer imaginable. Choosing a niche means focusing on something that your customers immediately recognize as serving them—making you stand out from your competitors.

In many cases, targeting a niche market will require little or no change to your actual products or services. You may just have to focus your marketing efforts on the specific group, perhaps changing some of your language and images to highlight that you serve a particular market.

Keep in mind that the word niche doesn't necessarily define the market as small, but rather, as specialized and identifiable by objective factors such as demographics, industry, activities engaged in, life stage, and so on. A niche is immediately understandable, such as:

- Hair care products for women with curly hair

- Bedding for people with allergies

- Accounting services specializing in serving dental practices

- Publisher specializing in entrepreneurship and business planning (that's PlanningShop)

Specializing may enable you to charge more for your products and services. That's because many customers will readily pay more for goods specially tailored for them, especially if those products or services are hard to find. Niche products and services also often generate powerful word-of-mouth activity.

Emphasize "shop small, shop local"

In a recession, customers tend to be more focused on low-cost than in boom times. Often, as a small business, your offerings may not be the least expensive so it's important to remind customers of why they feel good about purchasing from you, and make the fact that you're small and local—an important part of their community—a part of your marketing efforts.

- **Let customers know you are a small and local business.** Put that message on your signs, website, social media posts, take-out bags, and so on. It doesn't have to be clever; it just has to be frequent: "Your dollars support your local community."

- **Use social media tools for small business.** Instagram and other social media sites have created buttons to call out local and small businesses. Use those buttons yourself, encourage customers to use them, and call out to other local businesses.

- **Partner with other local companies.** Together, you can plan special events or marketing materials and have a better chance of getting local coverage for those activities.

- **Engage hyper-local media and local websites.** Small, very local papers depend on local businesses for their survival, so stay in touch with them and continually feed them stories about your business, other businesses in your neighborhood, and promotions and events you plan. Also, post promotions on hyper-local websites serving specific neighborhoods.

Business Terms Glossary

Advisory Committee: A non-official group of advisors; has no legal authority or obligation.

Angel: A private investor who invests personal funds in new enterprises.

Barriers to Entry: Conditions that make it difficult or impossible for new competitors to enter the market; examples include patents and extremely high startup costs.

Board of Directors: The governing body of an incorporated company; this body has legal authority and responsibility for the business.

Business Plan: A document outlining how a company will achieve its goals. A business plan can describe the concept and projected development of a startup company or the new product or project of an existing company. It assesses all critical aspects of a business—including its mission, market, industry, competition, team, operations, financials, objectives, and more—and identifies a sustainable strategic position.

Business Planning: The act of examining and researching the development of a new or existing company. Although the act of business planning doesn't necessarily require the creation of a written business plan, it does require an entrepreneur to rigorously evaluate and determine a company's fundamentals in order to successfully launch, grow, and even save a business.

Capital: Funds or money to establish or run a business.

Cash Flow: The movement of money into and out of a company; actual income received and actual payments made out.

Collateral: Assets pledged in return for loans; examples include real estate and accounts receivable.

Corporation: A legal form of business that provides certain benefits for the company's owners, including protection from personal liability.

Cost of Goods: The direct costs to make or acquire products being sold; examples include the cost of raw materials or inventory.

DBA: "Doing business as." A company's trade name rather than the name under which it is legally incorporated; a company may be incorporated under the name XYZ Corporation but do business as "The Dew Drop Inn."

Debt Financing: Raising funds for a business by borrowing, often in the form of bank loans.

Distributor: Company or individual that arranges for the sale of products from manufacturer to retail outlets; the proverbial "middle man."

Equity: Shares of stock in a company; ownership interest in a company.

Gross Profit: The amount of money earned after deducting the cost of goods but before deducting operating expenses.

LLC: Short for "Limited Liability Company," a specific legal form for a company providing limited liability and pass-through tax treatment for the company's owners.

Leasehold Improvements: Changes made to a rented store, office, or plant to make the location more appropriate for the conduct of the tenant's business.

Licensing Agreement: The granting of permission by one company to another to use its products, trademark, or name in a limited, particular manner.

Liquid Asset: An asset that can be turned into cash quickly and easily; examples include publicly traded stock and cash on deposit in banks.

Market Share: The percentage of the total available customer base captured by a specific company.

Milestone: A company's particular business achievement, such as shipping a new product or reaching a specific level of sales.

Net Profit: The amount of money earned after costs of goods and all operating and marketing expenses (often figured before taxes and depreciation).

Outsource: To have certain tasks done or products made by another company on a contract basis rather than having the work done by one's own company in-house.

Partnership: A relationship of two or more individuals to own or run a company without formal incorporation or the creation of an LLC.

Profit: The amount of money earned after expenses; it can be gross profit or net profit.

Profit Margin: The amount of money earned after expenses, usually expressed in percentage terms. *Gross profit margin* is the amount earned after deducting the cost of goods from total revenues; *net profit margin* is derived after deducting cost of goods plus operating expenses from total revenues.

Receipts: Funds coming into the company; the actual money paid to the company for its products or services; not necessarily the same as a company's total revenues.

Revenues: Total sales of a company before expenses. This is distinguished from profits or from receipts.

Sole Proprietorship: A non-incorporated company owned and managed by one person.

Strategic Partnerships: An agreement with another company to undertake business endeavors together or on each other's behalf.

Venture Capitalist: Individual or firm who invests money in new enterprises; typically this money is invested in the venture capital firm by others, particularly institutional investors.

Working Capital: The cash available to the company for the ongoing operations of the business.

Business Resources

Funding Sources

Angel Capital Association

www.angelcapitalassociation.org

Directory of groups of angel investors throughout the United States and Canada.

The Angels' Forum LLC

www.angelsforum.com

A group of angels that invests, mentors, and advises startups in Silicon Valley. Works with early stage companies from the seed stage through to the exit stage.

British Private Equity & Venture Capital Association

www.bvca.co.uk

The BVCA represents the vast majority of private venture capital firms in the United Kingdom.

Invest Europe

www.investeurope.eu

Based in Europe, Invest Europe is the largest association of venture capital firms in the world.

MAVA

www.mava.org

MAVA represents private equity and venture capital firms with investment interests in the Mid-Atlantic region and beyond.

National Association of Government Guaranteed Lenders

www.naggl.org

NAGGL is the association of banks and lending institutions that are active in offering SBA loans.

National Venture Capital Association

www.nvca.org

The NVCA represents the venture capital industry in the U.S. A list of member venture capital firms is available from the site.

Pratt's Guide to Private Equity & Venture Capital Sources

This long-standing annual directory lists more than 20,000 venture capital sources around the world. It lists contact information, recent investments, and capital under management, and is cross-referenced by investment preferences, investment stage, and other key information. It is very expensive to purchase—either online or in print—so check for availability at a good library.

The Red Herring

www.redherring.com

Website that tracks venture investing. Good insight and background on the venture capital community and recent deals.

Social Venture Circle

https://svcimpact.org

A network of investors making private investments to socially responsible companies. Apply (for a small fee) to make your pitch.

U.S. Small Business Administration (SBA)

www.sba.gov

Charged with the responsibility of aiding the cause of small businesses, the SBA maintains lists of banks and other lending institutions most active in making loans to small businesses in each geographical area. It also provides a loan guarantee program (not actual loans) to existing businesses, and direct loans limited to special categories such as Vietnam-era veterans and the disabled.

Westlake Securities

www.westlakesecurities.com

Westlake Securities provides a full range of investment banking and financial advisory services to emerging growth and established privately held and publicly traded companies.

Entrepreneurs' Sources

PlanningShop

555 Bryant Street, #180
Palo Alto, CA 94301
(650) 364-9120
fax: (650) 364-9125

www.PlanningShop.com

PlanningShop, the publisher of this book, is *the* central resource for business planning information and advice. At its website, you can purchase a downloadable template of Excel spreadsheets to match the financial worksheets in this book.

ASAE, The Center for Association Leadership

www.asaecenter.org

This national association of directors of trade, industry, and professional associations also provides a "Gateway" on its site that can help you locate associations related to your business.

Association of Small Business Development Centers

https://americassbdc.org

Over 1,000 SBDCs throughout the U.S. offer individual counseling, seminars, and technical help for entrepreneurs. Services are generally free. An outstanding, often overlooked, source of information for entrepreneurs.

Better Business Bureaus

www.bbb.org

A long-respected organization of businesses that agree to adhere to certain standards.

Edward Lowe Foundation

www.edwardlowe.org

Run by the Lowe Foundation, a nonprofit organization dedicated to assisting entrepreneurs. Extensive website of resources and articles.

Entrepreneurship.org

www.entrepreneurship.org

Developed and maintained by the private Kauffman Foundation, Entrepreneurship.org provides information on a wide variety of topics related to entrepreneurship and starting and running a business.

FWE: Forum for Women Entrepreneurs

www.fwe.ca

Founded in 2002, The Forum for Women Entrepreneurs (FWE) connects, educates, and supports women entrepreneurs across Canada through its various programs and events. Vancouver-based FWE supports 650 women each year.

Inc. Magazine and Website

www.inc.com

A leading magazine for growing business. Inc.'s website offers a substantial archive of articles on business issues.

NASE: National Association for the Self-Employed

www.nase.org

Membership organization providing a number of services to the self-employed and small businesses, including insurance and discounts.

NAWBO: National Association of Women Business Owners

www.nawbo.org

Membership group of women-owned businesses, with many local chapters around the country.

QuickBooks Community

https://quickbooks.intuit.com/learn-support/us-quickbooks-community/misc/03/community-us

Resources and peer-to-peer information sharing on small business topics, created by Intuit, maker of QuickBooks.

SCORE: Service Corps of Retired Executives

www.score.org

Provides retired business owners as counselors for assistance to individual entrepreneurs and conducts workshops on business skill topics.

SVForum

https://siliconvalleyforum.com

Long-standing, well-regarded group of Silicon Valley entrepreneurs, working primarily, though not exclusively, in high tech. Sponsors or cosponsors many seminars and programs on general entrepreneurship and startup issues. Conducts one-on-one meetings with venture capitalists.

Startup America

https://www.startupamericapartnership.org

Hundreds of founders, entrepreneurs, investors, mentors, and business executives work together to nurture startups throughout the U.S. Members become part of an extensive support network of startups, and gain access to valuable deals and resources from partner organizations.

Women in Technology International

www.witi.com

An organization devoted to increasing the number of women in executive roles in technology and technology-based companies. More oriented to employees than to entrepreneurs, but still a good source of information and excellent conferences. Has regional chapters.

Index

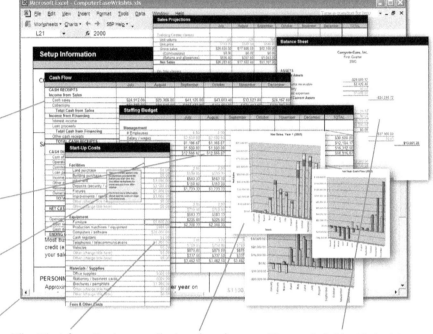

CPSIA information can be obtained
at www.ICGtesting.com
Printed in the USA
JSHW051423250321
12896JS00005B/5

9 781933 895864

Super Karate for Kids

Roger Carlon and Jane Hallander

UP Unique Publications
4201 Vanowen Place
Burbank, Ca 91505

First published in 2000 by Unique Publications

Library of Congress Catalog Number: 00-134272

ISBN: 0-86568-84-8

Distributed by:
Unique Publications
4201 Vanowen Place
Burbank, CA 91505
(800) 332–3330

Editor: Mark V. Wiley
Book Design: Patrick Gross

First edition
05 04 03 02 01 00 99 98 97 1 3 5 7 9 10 8 6 4 2
Printed in the United States of America

Contents

Introduction

Although there have been books written before that instruct adults how to teach the martial arts to children and young adults, never before has a comprehensive book been written *for* children and young adults to read and learn from. To this end, this book is written in language understandable to both young people and adults interested in learning the basics of most martial arts.

As an introduction, this book provides comprehensive information about the most popular basic fighting and self-defense techniques possible. The reader will notice only one chapter dealing with hand techniques, with most chapters giving instructions toward mastering the four basic kicking techniques. Since this book is intended for young readers, we wrote it toward keeping their interests in martial arts. In other words, everyone likes the challenge of perfecting kicks.

Again, geared toward the younger audience, we wrote the chapters with easy reference subtitles, making it easy to find any reference to techniques or pictures.

Since this book is designed to be used by young martial artist of any and all systems, the techniques described are common to most martial arts. Chapter One is a brief description of the most popular Asian martial arts. The chapters that follow deal with stretching and strengthening exercises; special training to develop the best kicks possible; the kicks themselves; kicking games; hand techniques; self-defense for children; and the mental aspects of martial arts studies.

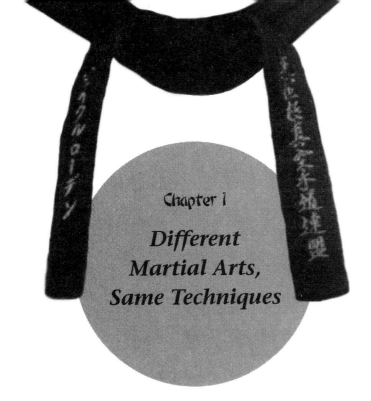

Chapter 1

Different Martial Arts, Same Techniques

The martial arts of Asian countries are as different as the countries themselves. Not only do martial artists wear different clothing styles, they do their forms differently, spar differently, and handle weapons differently. However, they all have one thing in common: the most effective techniques are basically the same, because there are only so many techniques that work well and fit our human bodies.

Let's now take a look at the martial art styles of different countries.

China

We commonly call China's martial art *kung-fu*. Actually the term kung-fu means *hard work*, not martial art. It's a term made popular during the Bruce Lee movie era, when Westerners were first exposed to his amazing fighting abilities. The real term for Chinese martial arts is either *wushu*,

which means *martial art*, or *koushu*, which translates to *national* or *military art*.

We often associate the term *wushu* with China's modern, acrobatic martial art, not with traditional Chinese martial arts. Therefore, for the sake of simplicity, we call China's traditional martial arts, *kung-fu*.

Martial arts from China are usually broken down into two categories—external and internal. External means martial styles that get their power from muscle and bone and require plenty of speed and physical strength to be effective. External Chinese martial arts are further divided into Northern and Southern styles. Southern Chinese systems include the southern Shaolin Temple arts, such as choy li fut, hung gar, wing chun, and hung fut. Northern Chinese external martial styles include northern Shaolin, chang chuan, and northern preying mantis, to name a few. These external Chinese martial arts all use speed, sheer physical strength and quick footwork to accomplish their goals.

The other type of Chinese kung-fu are the internal martial arts. They rely more on what the Chinese call *chou jing*, or *wise force*, to overcome their opponents. They actively combine *chi* energy, often considered our basic life-force energy, with muscle power to overcome an opponent. Arts such as tai chi chuan, hsing-i, pa kwa, and Chinese wrestling are the best known Chinese internal martial arts.

Chinese martial arts are known by their circular arm and hand movements. Northern styles also

have high, powerful kicks. Many Chinese arts imitate the fighting tactics of fierce animals, such as the tiger, leopard, preying mantis, and monkey.

Japan

Japanese martial arts are more straight line fighting styles, than the circular techniques of their Chinese cousins. Commonly called karate by those of us in the West, Japanese arts range from empty hand martial systems to joint locking and throwing systems to styles devoted entirely to weapons' practice.

The art of karate, which means *empty hand*, is commonly believed to have come to Japan from the island of Okinawa, where fighting with weapons was banned for many years. The Okinawans developed such an effective self-defense system that many Japanese masters wanted it as their own. It was brought to the Japanese mainland and became the best known Japanese martial art.

Before karate became well known in Japan, the most popular Japanese martial arts were kendo and ju-jutsu. Kendo means the *way of the sword* and is an art about Japanese samurai swordsmanship. These sword arts cover not only kendo, where heavily protected fighters spar with bamboo swords, but also kenjutsu, or swordsmanship, and iaido, or sword drawing and cutting from the scabbard to the first cut.

Ju-jutsu is a martial art that uses lots of joint

locks and throwing techniques to disarm and control an attacker. From the martial *art* of ju-jutsu came the martial *sport* judo. Judo was first developed in the early 1900s as the competition form of ju-jutsu. Judo is mainly a throwing art, similar to Chinese wrestling.

There are also Japanese martial arts that teach archery and special long weapons, such as the *naginata*, a long handled knife used mostly by women martial artists.

While karate doesn't look exactly like kung-fu, it still uses the same kicks and punches that makes kung-fu effective. Japanese martial arts, such as karate and ju-jutsu, use white uniforms, called a *gi*, and a colored belt system to determine students' rank within a school.

Korea

Korea is sandwiched between Japan and China. So, it only makes sense that Korean martial arts would look a little like both neighbors' arts. Many of the high kicks seen in tae kwon do resemble the high kicks of northern Shaolin, while tae kwon do punches look very close to karate punches.

Tae kwon do is the largest martial art in Korea. There are different stories about where tae kwon do came from, but the most import fact about it is that tae kwon do is 70% kicking techniques. That makes it both fun to do and difficult to master. Tae kwon do has recently become an Olympic medal

sport, which means it is now one of the most pop-ular martial arts in the world. Even the South Korean army loves tae kwon do, requiring all per-sonnel to study it throughout their time in their country's service.

Tae kwon do isn't the only martial art in Korea. There is tang soo do, a martial art that is supposed to have started in China. Hapkido is a popular joint locking and throwing art, closely resembling Japan's ju-jutsu. Kuk sool won is a combination of Chinese and Japanese influence, being the only Korean martial art that has kicking like tae kwon do, joint locks and throws similar to hapkido, and weapons training from ancient Korean martial arts.

Although tae kwon do is the best known and most popular Korean martial art, there are over 30 other Korean martial art systems. Korean arts, such as tae kwon do, also use uniforms called *dobak* to train in, and colored belts to show rank.

The training techniques in this book are designed to be used with most martial arts, because kicks and punches are important to mar-tial arts of any country.

Chapter 2

Warm-Ups & Stretches

Before you practice you need to warm up and stretch your muscles. Warming up is one of the fun parts of martial arts. It helps prevent injuries when you kick and punch. It also warms your muscles for better and easier stretches. Warm-up exercises are fun to do with other kids. You and your friends can start warming up by jogging or running around the martial arts school, in a line, with one person behind the other.

If you feel really good that day, do 50 jumping jacks after you finish running. Try to see who can jump the highest and clap their hands over their heads the loudest.

Another fun warm-up exercise is a special *hop*, where you hop straight up in the air three times in a row and *kiai* (or yell) on the third hop. Hop three times, count *one—two—three*, *kiai* and bring both knees to your chest as you do your kiai yell.

Finally, we need to warm-up the muscles around the *hips* and *knees*. Your hips are the joints

that control the height and power of all your kicks, so they must be loosened up before trying any serious kicks. The knees control the power and direction of the kick from the lower part of your leg. There are special warm-up exercises for the hips, called *hip rotations*. These are the basic lower back and hips warm-up exercises. For the legs we do *knee rotations*. Knee rotations help warm-up the muscles and ligaments that connect to your knees and also help prevent knee injuries.

Hip rotations are done from a stance where your feet are shoulders' distance apart. Put your hands on your hips and rotate your hips in 10 circles to the right, then 10 circles to the left.

To do *knee* rotations stand with your knees together. Place your right hand on the right knee and the left hand on the left knee. Then rotate both knees in a circle to the left 10 times and then to the right 10 times, keeping both hands on the knees as you do the warm-up exercise.

All Warmed Up
and Ready to Stretch

Why do we stretch our muscles before martial arts practice?

When we kick, we ask our muscles to extend as far as they can. If those muscles are not warmed up and stretched out, they can get small tears in the muscle fibers. These tears are what we call a *muscle strain* or, with bad tears, a *muscle*

9

Hamstring Stretch
Lean forward, back straight, legs spread apart and arms crossed.

sprain. When this happens all you can do is rest the torn muscle until it heals. When it does heal, it is never as strong as before the injury, because the tears are held together with *scar tissue* and scar tissue is weak connective tissue that is easily reinjured.

The first stretch to do is a stretch for your back and the backs of your legs *(hamstring muscles)*.

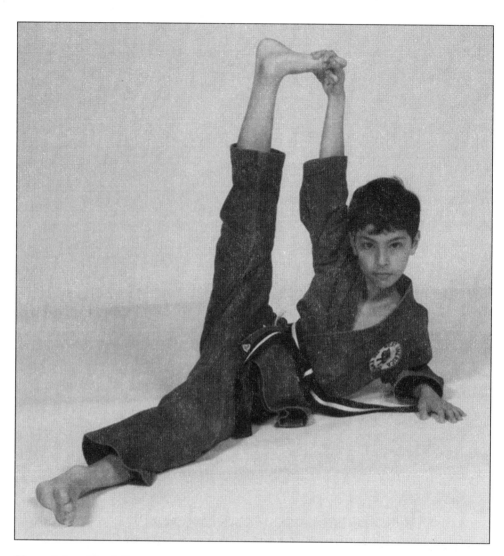

Hamstring Stretch
Lying on floor, one elbow down, with hand flat on the ground. Grab right foot with right hand and stretch as far back as possible.

Stand with your legs spread to about twice the width of your shoulders. While keeping your back and legs straight, lean forward as far as you can go. As you are doing this, make your arms form a circle in front of you, with the hands touching. This is actually a pre-stretch to make it easier to do the more difficult stretches that come next.

After you stretch your back with the first pre-stretch, you can do another pre-stretch for the hips and hamstring muscles. This stretch is done by propping one leg on something no higher than your own hips. Keep your back and both legs straight, as you lean forward toward the raised leg, as far as you can go. Your arms and hands will be in the same position as the back pre-stretch. Do both of these stretches for five to 10 minutes.

Next come the serious stretching exercises, where you stretch, as far as they will stretch the muscles, you are going to use in your martial art practice. However, it is important to remember that you should never feel any pain when you stretch. Stretching should always be fun and feel good.

A basic stretch is the *front stretch*. Sit on the floor with your legs spread as far apart as possible. Put your hands in front of you on the floor and lean as far forward as possible. Your hands will slide forward in the floor or mat. The ideal result is that you have your head and chest on the floor, with your legs as far to the side as possible. This is one of the best stretches for the lower back.

Hamstring Stretch for Basic Splits

Start with lead leg bent and back leg straight. Keep your back straight and both hands on the floor on each side of your body to keep your balance. Extend the lead leg slowly forward until you achieve the splits.

14

Front Stretch

Start with both legs spread as far apart as possible. Push against your knees, as you lean forward toward the floor. Grab one foot and pull yourself toward that foot. Then stretch to the other side, while pulling yourself toward that foot. Then lean forward until your chest touches the ground.

2

Partner Stretches

The most fun stretches are partner stretches. Stretching with a partner means that you and a friend can help each other get much better stretches than if you stretched by yourself. You can also control how much you stretch by asking your partner to either stretch a little further or stop if you have reached your limit.

Partner stretches are always done first with *tension*, followed by *relaxation*. The front stretch is a good one to start with. Stand with your back against a wall. Your partner holds one of your legs up off the ground in front of you. Have your partner push your leg upward until you feel the muscles start to resist, then tell him to hold your leg at that level. Push down with your raised leg against your partner's resistance. Then relax your raised leg and let your partner push it upward again, until the muscles tighten. Push down again against your partner's resistance. Hold your raised leg at its highest point for one minute. Stretch both legs like this, then do a *side kick* stretch.

Front Kick Partner Stretch

Side kick stretches are done the same as front stretches, except you will be facing to the left if stretching your left leg and to the right if stretching the right leg. If you are stretching your left leg, your right foot should be pivoted about 160 degrees away from the stretching left leg. When stretching your right leg for a side kick, turn your left foot about 180 degrees away from the right leg. When your leg reaches its highest level, tell your partner to stop pushing upward, and then push down for a count of 10 against his resistance. Stretch both legs. As you reach your highest point of the stretch, hold your stretched leg for 30 seconds to one minute. Don't let your buttocks stick out, keep your back straight and don't lean toward the stretching leg.

Front and side partner stretches make your hamstrings and hips more flexible to help you do higher front and side kicks.

Side kick Partner Stretches

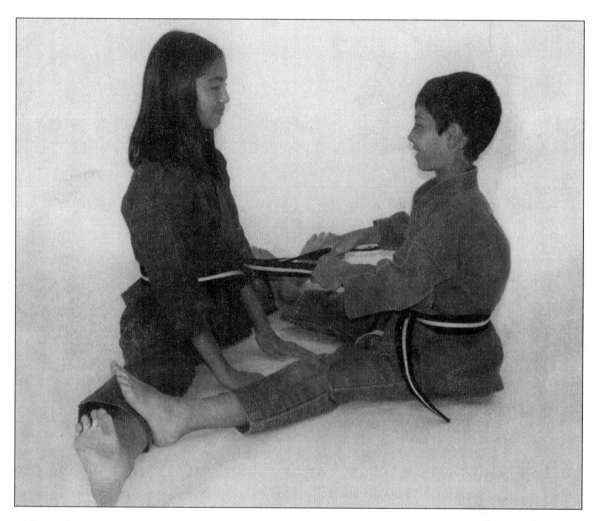

Side Kick Partner Stretch

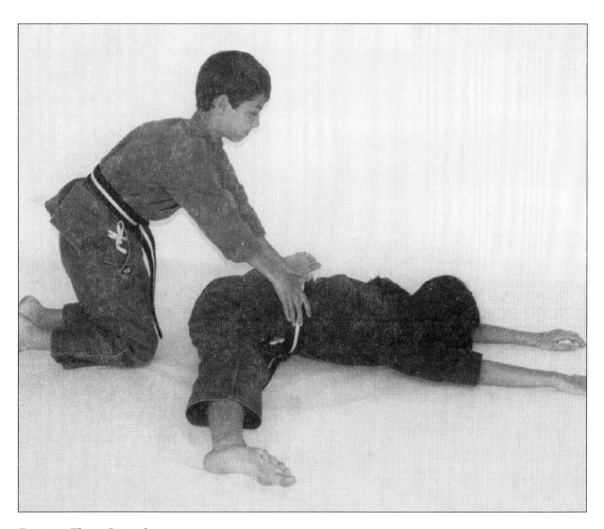

Partner Floor Stretch

For high kicks you must also stretch your hips. The *roundhouse kick* stretch is good for stretching your hips. Have your partner stand *behind* you and lift your bent leg. Keep your back straight. Your partner will lift your leg slightly toward your back. When you have reached the highest point of your stretch with your bent leg push down against your partner's resistance.

What if you don't have a partner to help you stretch?

Without a partner to help you stretch, you can put two pillows on the floor, one under each knee. Place both hands on the floor. Keep your feet apart, not together like a frog, and push back and forth with your hands flat on the floor to stretch your hips.

Friends and classmates can also help you do better front *splits*. Sit on the floor or mat with your legs spread as far apart as possible and put your hands on the floor in front of you. Then rotate your hips forward as if you were rolling them over a small log. Your training partner can help you by pushing your hips from behind you. This is an especially good stretch for loosening your hips. Loose, stretched hips are important for strong, high kicks.

Roundhouse Kick Partner Stretch

Chinese Splits Partner Stretch

2

3

Hamstring Stretch

30

2

It's Time to Strengthen Your Muscles

You need strong legs before you can have strong kicks. With one hand hold on to the wall to keep your balance. Have your partner raise your leg as far as it will lift comfortably, then have him let go of your leg and keep holding it up by yourself. Do this three times for each leg. Hold your leg up, in a kicking position, for five seconds each time or to a count of 10. Repeat with the other leg.

Then do the same thing with your partner in a side kick exercise. On the last leg lift, push upward a little farther than the lifts done before. It's good to do strengthening exercises three times a week.

You can have fun doing *squat* exercises to strengthen your *quadriceps muscles*. Strong quadriceps help you jump higher for jumping kicks. Squats are also fun to do with other classmates. Line up in a row, with everyone in a squat position. Then everyone jumps sideways to the right, landing in a squat position. Next, jump sideways back to the left and land in a squat. See who can jump the highest. Have one classmate hold a thin pole or Japanese *shinai* training stick a foot or two off the ground. Then hop sideways back and forth over the pole. The pole held by your partner or classmate makes a good obstacle to jump over. As you master jumping from a squat position over the pole, your partner raises it slightly, creating a challenge to jump higher.

You can also make squat exercises more difficult by jumping sideways and turning around 180 degrees, so that when you land you are facing the other direction. Do not let your buttocks touch the back of your heel when you are in the squat position. Doing that takes the *spring* out of your jump.

Squat Exercise Jumping over a Stick

**Squat Exercise Jumping
over a Stick Sideways**

Another fun squat exercise goes like this: squat first, then stand up and do a front kick, then back to the squat position, followed by another front kick, until you have done five front kicks. Or, you can start from a squat and stand up pivoting your body into a roundhouse kick. Follow this with a squat, then hook kick, and then a side kick.

With any kicks, other than front kicks, always squat, stand, and *pivot* before you do the kick. You don't have to pivot before the front kick

Squat Front Kick

because you don't turn your body. See who can put together the best variety of different kicks.

You can even practice jumping kicks from your squatting position. Start with the squat, then do a jumping front or roundhouse kick. Do not try to turn your body during the jump part of the kick when you do a squat, roundhouse kick. From the squat, stand up and turn your body to the side, then jump and do the roundhouse kick. Anyone can practice these simple exercises.

Squat Roundhouse Kick

4

5

42

1

2

Squat Side Kick

3

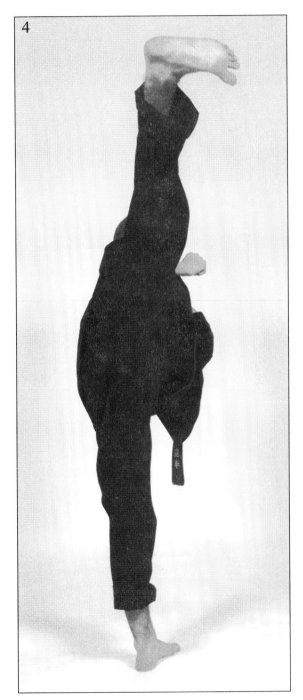

**Squat Jump
Roundhouse Kick**
*From a squatting
position, he leaps
into the roundhouse
kick.*

1

Squat Jump Front Kick
From a squatting position, he jumps into the front kick.

2

Side View

Squat Jump Side Kick
From a squat position, he jumps straight into a side kick.

1

2

Chapter 3

Chair Exercises & Slow Kicks

One reason we do *chair exercises* and *slow kicks* is to develop better balance. No one wants to do a beautiful kick, only to fall flat on their face when they bring their kicking leg down. Chair exercises are a fun and easy way to improve your posture and balance when kicking.

Chair Exercises

Front Kick

Stand next to a kitchen or folding chair, with the back of the chair on the opposite side of your kicking leg. If you are kicking with your right leg, hold the chair with your left hand. If kicking with the left leg, hold the chair with your right hand. If your chair is strong and sturdy, hold on to the middle of the chair-back. A weak or wobbly chair is best held at the forward end of the chair-back. First bring the knee of your kicking leg up into a cocked position, ready to kick. Then extend your kicking leg. Hold

your leg extended for a one, two and three count. Then cock it back with the knee bent, hold it for a one, two count, and lower it to the ground. Practice the front kick 10 times on each side. Remember to turn the chair around and repeat with the other leg. The chair should always be on the opposite side of your kicking leg.

Front Kick

3

4

5

Roundhouse Kick

The chair position for roundhouse kicks is the same as for a front kick. Raise your kicking leg, cock the knee, then extend the leg into the kick, cock your knee again, hold the knee cocked for a one count, and drop the leg down to the ground. When you extend your leg into the kick, hold it for a one, two, three count. Then bring your knee back to a cocked position and hold it for a one, two count. Do your roundhouse kick 10 times on each side.

A common mistake with round-house kicks is dropping the kicking leg straight down after the kick. Instead, a good roundhouse kick finishes with a circular motion, bringing the cocked leg back to its starting position.

Roundhouse Kick

56

Side Kick

The side kick exercise is done the same as the front and roundhouse kicks. First lift the kicking leg with your knee cocked, then extend your leg for the side kick. Hold your leg in its side kick position for a one, two, three count, then cock it back, hold it in the cocked position for a one, two count, and drop it to the ground

Side Kick

Hook Kick

Hook kicks begin looking like side kicks, however that changes when the kicking leg is extended into the hook kick. As soon as the leg is extended, it travels 45-degrees outward, away from your body, then cocks back for a one, two count. It is then brought to the ground with a circular movement, like a roundhouse kick. The hook kick's direction is opposite of a roundhouse kick, moving clockwise, or away from your body, rather than counter-clockwise across your body as a roundhouse moves. Both side and hook kicks pivot the stationary foot farther than does a roundhouse kick. This causes your hips to rotate farther and brings the knee of your kicking leg past your opponent.

Roundhouse kicks have the knee pointed toward the target. Side and heel kicks bring the knee about 45 degrees past the target's direction, then extend the foot to have the heel of the kicking foot pointing at the target or opponent.

As your balance gets better, you can start practicing kicks without the chair. If you want a challenge, do all

Hook Kick

kicks—front, side, heel, and round-house—without dropping your leg down to the ground. Count one, two, and three for each kick extension and do five sets of the four basic kicks for each leg. If you have a portable folding or full-length mirror you can watch yourself practice and correct your kicking form as you practice. You might also hold the chair and do all of your kicks as fast as you can as a warm-up exercise for more serious practice.

3

4

5

6

Slow Kicks

When you can easily do your four basic kicks with a chair for balance, it is time to graduate to *slow kicks*. Slow kicks are the same techniques, done without the chair. They are the kicks that you will someday do at full speed. They are first practiced slowly to develop better balance and stronger leg muscles. Also, if you cannot do your kicks correctly at slow speed, you cannot do them fast.

It is best to face a mirror when you practice slow kicks. With a mirror, you can easily correct mistakes, learn to position your body correctly and correctly pivot your stationary foot.

Here are a few basic rules for good slow kicks.

1) Always start from a fighting position, with your hands up in guard position and both knees bent. For instance, the front kick is done the same as with a chair, except instead of holding the chair, your hands are now part of your kicking technique. The front kick has the same knee lift and cock, leg extension, cock back to the same one, two count, and drop the leg to the ground.

However, the hand movements are different

Slow Side Kick

from chair kicks, because you don't have to hold the chair. The hands follow your kicking leg. When you start the kick, your left hand is forward. When you pick up your right leg for the actual kick, your right hand follows and comes forward, replacing the left hand. This hand movement is the same for each kick. A good kicker will not move either hand back for balance. Your balance is best if both hands are kept close to your body.

2) Start your slow kicks with both legs bent. After you pivot into the kick your supporting leg becomes completely straight. This gives you better balance and more power for your kick. If you start to lose your balance, don't give up. Instead, fight it and try to keep your balance. You will develop better balance by fighting to keep your balance than if you stop and start over. Keep your kicking leg's knee high for better balance, as you cock the leg before and after the kick. Do not drop your leg until you have finished the cock back after the kick.

4   Or

5   Or

64

1

Slow Back Kick

2

3

Slow Spin Hook Kick

4

5

6

7

8

Chapter 4

Basic Kicks at Regular Speed

There are two kinds of kicks: snap and thrust. Front, side, and roundhouse kicks can be done as both thrust and snap kicks. Hook kicks are snap kicks only. Since hook kicks are arcing kicks that require a circular action to complete the kick, it is impossible to do them as thrust kicks.

Snap kicks are valuable for controlling kicking force and accuracy while sparring. If you are sparring and make contact with a snap kick, you will not hurt your partner. Thrust kicks are used to penetrate when you are breaking boards, for developing strong power, and in self-defense situations. Thrust kicks have less control than snap kicks, but have much more power than the faster snap kicks. Whether they are snap or thrust kicks, your kicks should now be done as fast as possible.

1

2

Front Kicks

While front snap kicks performed slow are done to the count listed in Chapter Three, when you do front kicks at fast speeds you should pick your kicking leg up and cock the knee in the same movement. The count for a front snap kick is also changed. Pick up and cock for a one count, extend the leg into the front kick for a one count, then cock back for one count before dropping the foot to the ground. Front thrust kicks have the kick extended for a longer period of time—a one, two, three count.

All types of kicks should have the knee of the kicking leg held in a comfortable position. Do not drop down lower during the cock back after the kick. The knee stays at the same height as when you do the kick.

Front Kick

3

4

Or

Roundhouse Kicks

Roundhouse kicks are performed the same as listed in Chapter Three and when done fast with the same count as front kicks. However, both snap and thrust roundhouse kicks should always hold the final knee cocked back, because you often want to kick again with another technique.

Roundhouse Kick

3

4

Or

Hook Kick

Hook Kicks

Hook kicks start with the knee cocked, like a side kick, and finish cocked like a roundhouse kick. After starting like a side kick, hook kicks extend the kicking leg at a 45 degree angle, then hook back to a cocked knee position that resembles a roundhouse kick's cocked knee. There is no *thrust* hook kick, only snap hook kicks. Hook kicks are fast moving, penetrating kicks that take an opponent down with power generated from their speed and accuracy.

Both hook and side kicks have very fast lift and cock knee actions. The supporting foot pivots into kicking position as the kicking leg lifts and cocks at the knee. Try to see how fast you can do the lift, cock, and pivot—all at the same time. After the kick, hold the final cock back for a count of one, two, three, then drop the leg down.

5

6

7

8

Kicking Speed

The best formula for speed is *practice*. The more you practice any one technique, the faster you will become at it. Speed with kicking techniques comes not from how fast you get your leg up, but how fast you can extend your leg into the actual kick.

Sliding Kicks

Sliding Front Kick

Sliding forward into a kick—rather than *stepping* into a kick—has the advantage that you stay the same level, not bobbing up and down as most people do when they try to step forward and kick. Sliding the foot is fast, smooth, and keeps your energy continuous, right up until you start the actual kick.

Sliding kicks should start from a long stance, which means you will cover more ground as you slide into your kicking position. A long stance means you will slide and kick, rather than step, slide, and kick, making your kicking technique much faster and smoother.

Sliding kicks include the four basic kicks—front, roundhouse, side and hook kicks. Sliding kicks, with the exception of front kicks, start from a medium width, square stance position. Sliding

front kicks start from a forward stance, with one leg in front of the other.

As a sliding kick starts, the front foot slides forward as the back foot comes up to kick. This makes it look almost like a slide, hop, and kick technique. When you first learn sliding kicks, do them in this sequence—step together, cock the kicking leg, and kick. You should turn your hip and knee further for hook and side kick sliding kicks, much the same as when doing slow kicks.

A fast sliding roundhouse kick always has a small *hop* that places you in a 180-degree pivot position, rather than the regular step, pivot, and kick of a stationary roundhouse kick.

Sliding side kicks are always locked out as thrust kicks.

4

Sliding Roundhouse Kick
Chantel Carlon starts from a ready position, slides her back foot forward to a position next to the kicking foot, launches a high roundhouse kick, cocks her kicking leg back and steps down to the ready position.

3

4

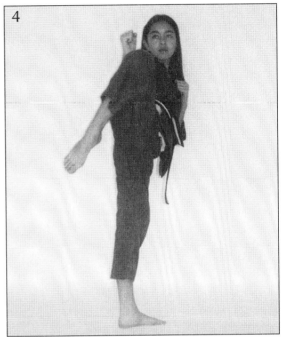

5

Sliding Hook Kick
After first sliding forward, Roger Carlon Jr. cocks his kicking leg, launches the hook kick, and cocks his leg back after the kick.

3

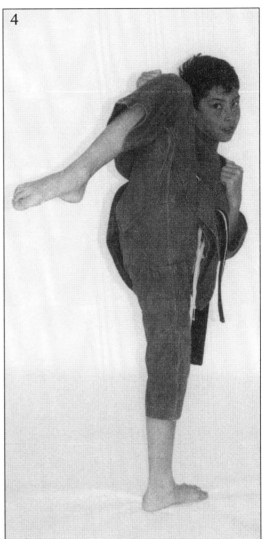

4

Sliding Side Kick
Chantel Carlon in ready position, slides her back foot forward to the front leg and cocks her kicking leg. She launches the side kick and cocks the kicking leg back after the kick is finished.

Chapter 5

Turning & Spinning Kicks

Spinning kicks are among the flashiest and most powerful of all kicking techniques. There are few sights more exciting than the whirling action of a kicker a few seconds before he connects with his target. However, before you can fill those kicking shoes, you must learn *turning* kicks, especially the 360-degree turning kick.

Although we call it a turning kick, the 360-degree kick is actually somewhere between a sliding and spinning kick. It is a technique that turns you around in a full circle.

360-Degree Front and Roundhouse Kicks

The 360-degree front kick is an offensive or attacking technique. Like the front sliding kick, your forward leg is always the kicking leg. The difference is, front sliding kick techniques do not turn around, while you turn completely around with a 360-degree kick.

1

Start from a fighting stance, with your left leg forward. Then turn in a 360-degree circle to the left (counter-clockwise), pivoting on your right leg, and kick with the left leg. This is an attack kick, because there is no reason to use it defensively. It's a surprise technique, commonly used when your opponent thinks you are going to kick with your back leg.

Don't lift the turning leg too high and keep the length of your stance the

2

3

360-Degree Front kick

same when you land as when you start the kick. This applies to all 360-degree kicks. When you do a 360-degree front or roundhouse kick, turn in a full counterclockwise circle, then kick.

A 360-degree roundhouse kick has the same turn as a 360-degree front kick, however the stationary foot must pivot 160- to 180-degrees after the initial turn.

4

1

3

2

4

360-Degree Roundhouse Kick

5

6

7

360-Degree Hook Kicks

As you do a 360-degree hook or side kick, turn clockwise until you are facing the opposite direction, look at your target, and execute your hook or side kick.

360-Degree Hook Kick
From a ready position, Roger Carlon Jr. turns around 360 degrees, then cocks his kicking leg. Then he launches the kick, then cocks his leg back.

Spinning Kicks

The principle of spinning kicks is defense against an opponent who is attacking from the front. To do a good spinning technique you should look at the target as you turn around. At the same time cock the knee of your kicking leg and launch the spin kick. Immediately after the kick, cock your leg and come back around to your original position. Since spinning kicks are difficult techniques, you should practice them slowly, before you try them at full speed.

There is no need for a spinning front kick because spin kicks are usually defensive kicks. They are used as offense techniques only if you are sparring and the opponent is not moving and you need an opening technique to start the action.

As defensive techniques, spin kicks are used as the opponent comes toward you. A well-done spin kick has enough speed and power to not only stop the opponent, but act as a counter attack.

The only spinning kicks are hook and back kicks. There's also another type of spinning back kick called a reverse side kick. A reverse side kick is actually a turning side kick. The regular spinning back kick comes from the ground as if it were a lifting kick, without cocking the knee. A reverse side kick is done by cocking the knee like a regular side kick, spinning 180-degrees, and kicking as if it were a back kick with the side of the foot making contact.

The spinning back kick should be learned before the reverse side kick. Get used to turning

your head and pivoting at the same time. Kick from the ground, without cocking your knee. After you master the spinning back kick, you can start cocking the knee for the reverse side kick.

Start facing your imaginary opponent, with your hands in a fighting guard position. Keep the same hand position throughout the entire kick. Turn your head to keep looking at the opponent and pivot on both feet 180-degrees. Focus on the target, kick from the ground if it's a back kick, or cock the knee for a reverse side kick. Do the kick. Then bring your kicking leg back to the ground in a ready position. If you've just done a reverse side kick, cock the knee back after the kick, and then drop it to the ground.

When you do a spinning back kick, start your spinning action with the kicking leg still on the ground. The knee cocking starts as the kicking leg starts extending, making the spinning back kick more of a straight line kick than its look-alike reverse side kick.

One way to test the power and accuracy of your spinning kicks is to have your training partner hold a body shield or X-ray paper. If you're doing a spinning hook kick, have your classmate hold two targets to kick through, rather than one. With two targets to kick through you won't stop your kick before you finish the hooking motion. X-ray paper is good to use, because it makes a loud noise when it's kicked. You always know when you've done a good kick.

There are two ways to do a good spinning hook kick. The first way is by cocking your kicking leg before starting the spin. Then spin around and kick. The second way is faster, but takes more practice. The faster method has you cock your knee *as* you spin, then kick.

A good hook kick will have the leg extended immediately after cocking the knee, but before the kick is executed. Don't try to extend your leg as you are doing the actual hooking action.

One common mistake made with spinning kicks is rotating the body too far, without pivoting. Not focusing on the target can cause you to over rotate. Spinning kicks should be executed at the *end* of your 180-degree pivot.

1

Spinning Hook Kick

3

4

5

6

Chapter 6

Jumping Kicks

If you cannot reach your targets with a standing kick, you can often reach them with a jumping kick. In ancient times martial arts kicks were used against people standing on the ground and against people riding horses. In those days there were no guns or cars and martial artists sometimes had to reach a person mounted on a horse. One way to do that was with a jumping kick.

Jumping kicks are the martial arts' glamour kicks. They are the kicks everyone wants to do well. However, sometimes people do ask: "Why should we learn to do jumping kicks? They are flashy, but if I can kick to someone's head with a standing kick, why should I jump?"

One reason jumping kicks are valuable is that they are always aimed at higher targets than regular kicks. If you cannot kick high with a stationary kick, you can always jump to get extra height and reach your target.

Jump Front Kick
He starts from a standing ready position and jumps straight into a high front kick.

How do you build up your body strength to perform a good jump kick? There are two important muscle groups that lead to powerful, high jump kicks—calves and quadriceps. These are the muscles you want to strengthen for good jumping kicks.

Strong calves are developed by holding on to a chair for balance, with one foot locked behind the knee of the other leg. Then straighten up all the way to the tip of the toes of your standing foot. Slowly lower yourself to a regular standing position with your stationary foot flat on the ground. Do this up and down exercise 10 times on each leg.

Squat Jumps

You can strengthen quadriceps muscles by doing *squat jumps,* where you jump over an object, such as a long stick held by a classmate. Squat jumps are done by first dropping into a squat position, then jumping straight over the object.

As you become better at squat jumps, try squatting first, then turning your body as you jump over the object. Squat all the way, then twist your body a full 360-degrees, and jump over the obstacle. You can also squat first, then jump from side to side over a target, or jump and turn and land on the other side, facing the opposite direction. Do 10 squat jumps with each leg.

Squat Kicks

Next, work up to doing all basic kicks from a squat position, without moving.

Keep your body and back straight as you do a series of 10 squat kicks. Practice the four basic kicks. If you have a knee injury, squat only half way down with each squat exercise. This means you first squat, then stand up and kick. You can do hook and side kicks from a squat starting position, then stand up, pivot, and kick. When you practice squat kicks make sure you go all of the way down into a full squat and come up and kick—unless you have knee problems, then only do a half squat.

Squat Jumping Kicks

Do the same exercise with squat, jump, and kick—
10 times on each leg for each kick. Practice these
exercises three times a week. When you do squat
exercises do not touch your buttocks to your heel.
Your thighs should be no lower than parallel to the
ground. If you go lower, you may injure your
knees. Both basic standing and jumping kicks can
be done from a squat position.

Basic Jumping Kicks

Jumping kicks should not be done from a long
stance. Shoulder's length is as long as your stance
needs to be for good jumping kicks. If your stance
is too long, you will have to take an extra step into
your kick.

There are four basic jumping kicks: jump
front, roundhouse, hook, and side kicks—all done
with either the lead or back leg.

When you do a jumping front leg front kick,
keep your body aimed straight at the target.
However, jumping front leg roundhouse kicks have
your body turned toward the side. This is the same
position for jumping front leg hook and side kicks.
Only front and side jumping kicks are thrust kicks.
Hook and roundhouse kicks are always snap kicks.

A jumping front kick with the back leg kick
starts with a squat, then jump and kick, with the
other leg tucked tightly against your buttocks.

Tucking the leg that isn't kicking, during a jump kick, gives your kick more height. When the kicking leg is extended, the other leg should be cocked up as close to your body as possible. Your non-kicking or supporting leg should never hang down while you are kicking, because that makes you land too soon and you cannot kick very high.

One Step Jump Side Kick
He starts from a ready position, takes a step forward, and kicks.

112

3

360-Degree Jumping Kicks

360-degree jumping kicks are similar to 360-degree standing kicks, except that with a 360-degree jumping kick you will turn around in a full circle, *without* traveling forward, as you do with a regular 360-degree kick. Stationary 360-degree kicks use a forward step because you are chasing an opponent.

Jump Side Kick against a Body Shield Target
From a standing position, he jumps straight up to a high side kick.

While the basic 360-degree kicks are the same four front, roundhouse, hook, and side kicks, there is no front jumping 360-degree kick. All 360-degree side kicks should be done against a target, such as a body shield. Jumping back kicks are also practiced against body shields.

2

Jump Spinning Kicks

The only jump spinning kicks are hook and back kicks. Jump spinning hook and jumping reverse side kicks, or back kicks, start from an upright fighting position. Next, bend your knees into a squatting position and look over your shoulder at the target. From the squat position, jump as high as you can, with both legs cocked as tight as possible, extend your kicking leg. The reverse side kick extends straight, while the hook turns your body 45-degrees as it follows the hook kick.

Jumping Back Kick

When you do a jump spinning hook or back kick, jump up, spin, and then return to your starting position. Be sure your kicking leg is cocked as much as it will bend to deliver a good kick. A jump spinning hook kick carries your body all the way around in a full circle. When practicing jump spinning hook kicks use two sheets of X-ray paper, as they forces you to extend your leg to the side of the target, creating a hooking action in order to kick both papers. Without two targets, you may kick straight, rather than hook their kicking leg.

2

Chapter 7

Kicking Games

A good way to develop strong, fast kicks is by playing *kicking games*. These are games that you can play with your class-mates in a friendly, competitive manner. Kicking games involve multiple kick combinations, series of one kick repeated many times, kicks done in many different directions, and kicks repeated at different heights. What most kicking games have in common is that they are multiple kicks done with-out dropping your kicking leg to the ground. The game is to see who can do the most without putting the foot down.

Multiple Kick Combinations

Multiple kicks, such as roundhouse, hook, and side kicks, are combinations where you do two or more kicks without putting the kicking leg down. A fun and interesting way to practice fast multiple kicks, up to 10 at a time, is where you hold your

kicking leg's knee at the same level for all of the kicks, and see who can do the most kicks without dropping the leg to the ground.

You might also do combinations of different basic kicks to different angles. For instance, you could do roundhouse, side kick, roundhouse, and roundhouse kicks in different directions. It might turn out like this: the first roundhouse kick to the left, then turn to the right for the side kick, back to the right for the third roundhouse kick, and to the left for the last roundhouse. That itself is difficult. However, you can make it even more challenging by repeating the combination until you can no longer hold that kicking leg off the ground.

Another variation of multiple kick combinations is kicking to different heights. For example, low, medium, and high kicks, or whatever height combinations you want to use. Then turn it into a game by seeing who can do the greatest number of height combinations before their leg tires.

Repeating One Kick

Another kicking game is to see who can do the most of one type of kick, such as front or roundhouse kicks. You cannot repeat hook kicks, however you can alternate hook and roundhouse kicks together, or combinations like hook, roundhouse, and side kicks, making it into a multiple kick combination game. Pick a certain combination, then see who can do the greatest number of that combi-

nation, before dropping the leg. This can also be done as a hook and side kick combination.

Sometimes it is fun to do a series of snap roundhouse kicks. You don't have to compete with a classmate with this game. Do up to five snap roundhouse kicks in a row. Sometimes these are called *machine gun* kicks. You might also do three or more thrust side kicks in a row, or as you get better at multiple kicks, three snap side kicks, followed by three thrust side kicks.

Another useful game is called *roundhouse kick arounds*. These are roundhouse kicks done continuously in a circle. Do them first in one direction, then in the other direction.

You can also hop forward in a straight line, while kicking continuously with the other leg. This game tests your balance and ability to do two things at one time.

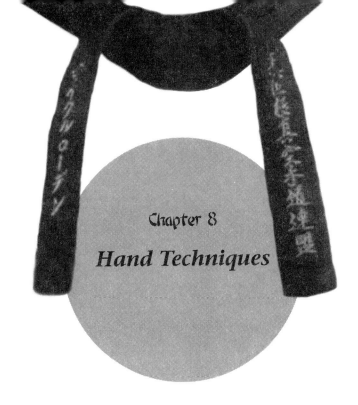

Chapter 8

Hand Techniques

While kicking is fun, lively and very powerful, *hand* techniques are an important part of every martial art. You can be the best kicker in your school, but if you haven't mastered your art's hand techniques, you will never be a complete martial artist. The following are basic hand techniques for most martial arts.

Punches

Punches, or fist techniques, always start from a fighting stance position. The fist is usually made by folding your four fingers tight against the palm of your hand. Your thumb is then folded across the first two fingers—index and middle fingers. This is the most common fist position in martial arts. It not only gives you a strong punch, but also protects your hand and fingers from injury when you hit the target.

1

Lead Punch

Lead Hand Punch

The first punch is a *lead hand* punch or *front* punch, called a jab in boxing. Start from a shoulders-width fighting stance, with your right leg and right hand forward. Keep your knees bent. Your right hand, which is in the lead, delivers the punch. It is important that your shoulder, waist, and hips extend and lead your fist into the punch. The punching hand for a front or lead hand punch is the same hand as your forward foot.

Lead Punch with partner

Reverse Punch

The *reverse* punch is a straight punch, done with the *opposite* hand as the forward leg. If your left leg is forward, you will punch with the right hand. The main difference between the front punch and reverse punch is that you must pivot on the ball of your back foot with a reverse punch. This pivot allows your body to turn toward the punch and its target and gives you much more power. As you punch, your back heel will lift off the ground. You will also extend your punching hip and shoulder toward the target.

Reverse Punch

130

Reverse Punch with partner

132

Back Fist

Back Fist Punch

The third basic punch is the *back fist,* a fist attack that comes to the target at a slight angle and makes contact with the knuckles on the back of your hand. When doing a back fist, always keep your elbows pointed downward and close to your body. Extend your hand into the back fist as you lean forward toward the target. In school sparring, because you wear a helmet, back fists are aimed at the side of the opponent's head where little damage can be done.

134

Back Fist with partner

Upper Cut Punch

Finally there is the *uppercut* punch, which is a fist attack that moves *under* the opponent's guard hand. It is a rear hand technique only. If your left foot is forward, your right hand delivers the uppercut punch. The uppercut punch is a lifting technique, used only for close distance sparring or fighting. There is very little arm extension with an uppercut punch. However, you do need to turn your body to put power into the punch. To do that, pivot on the ball of your back foot as you do with a back fist technique, finishing with your back heel raised.

Sliding Punches

There are two fist techniques that can be done with *sliding* footwork: sliding back fist and sliding reverse punch. The hand actions are the same as done from a stationary stance. What makes sliding punches effective is the quick, forward movement of your footwork. When you do sliding footwork, push off with your back foot, step forward with the front foot, and land in the same stance as you started from. Don't finish your sliding step with your feet together, because you can easily lose your balance in that position.

A sliding reverse punch starts with the same footwork as the sliding back fist, however finishes with the back foot pivoting and the heel raised, just like a regular reverse punch.

Shuffle Punches

Shuffle footwork is a very fast reversal of forward foot, done to confuse your opponent. An opponent who expects your punch to come from a certain hand is instantly confused when you change your stance position with shuffle footwork. As with sliding punches, there are only two basic punches used with shuffle footwork—shuffle back fist and shuffle reverse punch.

When you do a shuffle back fist, you are striking the target with your forward hand, the same hand as your forward foot. The shuffle footwork is done by crossing forward with your back foot and punching as you are moving.

For a shuffle reverse punch you will actually switch forward legs with a quick hopping motion, followed by the reverse punch.

Open Hand Techniques

The two basic open hand techniques are *ridge hands* and *palm strikes.* Ridge hands, like back fists, are aimed toward the side of the opponent's head. However, palm strikes are targeted to the opponent's nose or face.

Ridge Hand Strikes

Ridge hands are the hook kicks of punches. They are divided into front hand and rear hand actions. To do a good front hand ridge hand strike, pivot on your forward leg to turn your body 45-degrees away from your target. This places you in a good position to deliver a strong ridge hand strike. The

Front Hand Ridge Hand

ridge hand is made with the thumb bent into a safe position next to your palm. Your fingers are angled back and away from the target. Hit the target with the inner edge of your hand, just above the wrist. Rear hand ridge hand techniques are done the same as a reverse punch, by pivoting on the ball of the back leg and lifting the back heel.

Back Hand Ridge Hand

3

Palm Strikes

Palm strikes are the other common open hand techniques. They are also divided into front hand and rear hand attacks. There is no difference between palm strikes and punches, except your hand is open. The striking surface of a palm strike is the entire palm and heel of the hand. Palm

Palm Strike

strikes are dangerous techniques that have no place in school sparring classes. Palm strikes are strictly for self-defense.

Chapter 9

Self-Defense

I f you ever need to use your martial arts for your own defense, remember this basic advice: kicks used in self defense should not be higher than your attacker's chest. If you use kicks when sparring *always* kick higher than waist level.

Kicking Techniques

The safest, most effective kicks for self-defense are kicks to the attacker's chest, knee, shin, or instep. Those areas are easy to reach and are painful. Also, you are less likely to lose your own balance if you kick to an attacker's knee, than if you try a higher kick to his head or upper body. Since it takes longer to kick high than it does to kick low, kicks to the knee or lower are fast and hard to counter.

In a tournament sparring match you must kick above belt level because sparring matches are not meant to injure one another. Most tournament rules allow only kicks above the waist or belt level.

Here are a few good self defense applications for the techniques you have already learned in this book.

If someone grabs you and pulls you forward, toward them, you can make them let go of their grab with a front kick to their knee or groin area. You might also do a low side kick to the shin, or a roundhouse kick with your instep to the attacker's knee or thigh.

The side of an attacker's knee is another good target. A roundhouse kick with either front or back

Defense against a wrist grab.
From a wrist grab, Chantel Carlon front kicks her attacker in the groin area.

1

leg to the side of the attacker's knee will make
your assailant let you go, allowing you to run
away. Another way to make an attacker let go of a
grab is a front kick to the groin, done with either
your leading leg or rear leg.

If you are grabbed from behind, do a back
kick stomping foot technique to your attacker's
instep. Another good defense for a grab from
behind is a side kick to the shin that scrapes down
the attacker's shin, until it reaches his instep and
becomes a stomping kick.

Self-defense against a grab can be a well-aimed side kick.

2

Against a front choke Chantel strikes the attacker's throat.

*Defense against a choke from behind might be a back kick
to the attacker's shin.*

Ground Techniques

If you have been thrown to the ground, or lose your balance and fall, you can do several kicks in a row from your position on the ground. Make sure you yell as loud as you can while you are defending yourself.

Roundhouse to the knee

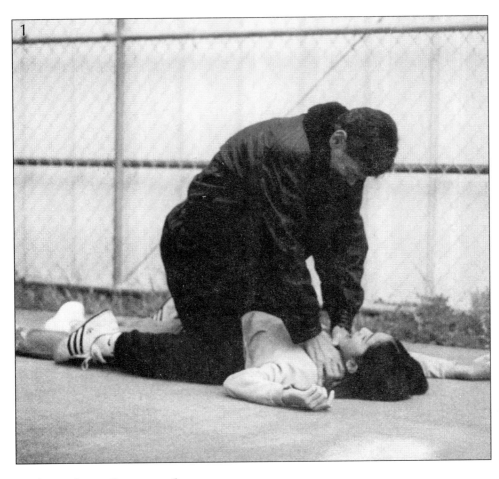

Defense from the ground.
While being choked, Chantel Carlon reaches up and pulls him off her by rolling over to one side, she then attacks his face.

156

2

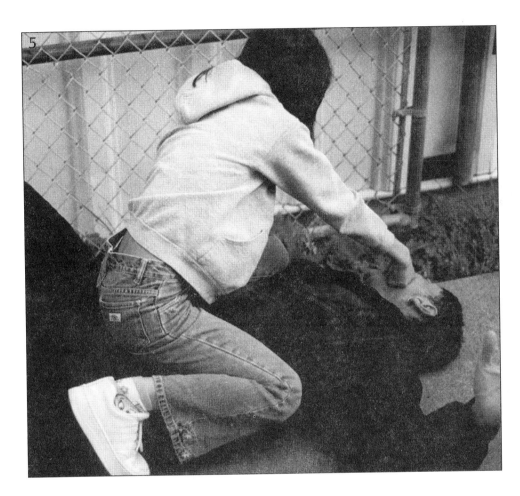

Hand Techniques

The best hand technique for instant self-defense is a palm smash to the attacker's nose. This not only makes him let go, but causes pain and light-head-edness, disorienting him and giving you a perfect chance to escape. Another good hand technique is a poke into the attacker's eye with the tips of your fingers. This is useful if you are grabbed and lifted off the ground. You can use either your fingers in the attacker's eyes or your elbow to his face. Your elbow is a great weapon in a close range self-defense situation.

Most attackers do not protect their throat. They try to protect their groin or their face, forgetting that one of the most vulnerable areas of the body is the throat. A sharp strike to the throat can cause pain and loss of breath, or even the windpipe to col-lapse. The best way to hit the throat is by making a V between your thumb and index finger—called the *web* of the hand—and hitting low on the attacker's throat with the center of this V shape.

When choked, Chantel Carlon counters with a hand strike to the throat.

Chapter 10

Body, Mind & Spirit

Martial arts start and end with *respect,* for both physical and mental aspects. In order to master your body you must also master your mind and spirit. If you don't master body, mind, and spirit you are not an accomplished martial artist.

In the previous chapters we talked about your physical workout. Now it is time to cover the mental aspect of martial art training. For instance, why do we bow?

Bowing before sparring, forms practice, stretching, or to your teacher is a polite way to acknowledge your respect for your classmates, martial arts school, and instructor.

Respect

Respect extends beyond bowing. When we spar we must respect the sex, age and size of our opponent. If the school's master is sparring with a much lower

ranked student, he or she should not use the same techniques and intensity in the same way as if sparring with another black belt. White belt fighters should not attempt to *prove* themselves by overcoming their teachers, especially since the instructor is demonstrating his respect for you. Higher degree rank respects lower rank and vice versa.

Sparring should always be a pleasant experience. It doesn't always have to be a win or lose situation. Sparring's goal should be to develop new techniques each time you spar. Don't rely on one or a few of your favorite techniques all of the time. Try to be versatile.

Patience

It takes patience to learn to fight well. It takes patience to get to black belt level. Some say it takes practicing 1,000 times to master some forms or kicks.

Each martial art has different ranking systems, based on ability, attitude, and class attendance. Have the patience to accept the fact that you must master your techniques before moving on to higher ranks within your art.

Determination

Don't ever give up in your martial arts training, even if you sometimes feel frustrated with your performance. If you have the will to do whatever

you want to do and don't give up, you will be successful. Always keep trying. Your determination with your martial arts training will carry over into your school and life.

Loyalty

Loyalty means being "faithful to a cause or ideal." Your martial art is your cause and ideal. A true martial artist is faithful to his or her art, school, teacher, and classmates. Like everything else in martial arts, loyalty extends into everyday life.

Sharing

Sharing means sharing knowledge with your classmates and others. Helping your classmates is an important part of martial arts. Remember, there are two words in martial arts. *Martial* describes the physical side. *Art* is your personal growth.

Attitude

Attitude is your mental feeling or belief in something. Your attitude should be humble and yet positive. Someone with a good attitude who wins first place at a tournament doesn't brag about it to his classmates. Instead, he accepts his win with pride and humbleness, giving credit to his teacher, school, and martial art. A good attitude carries over into daily life.

Self-Control

Mental self-control is important when you are sparring. You should never lose your temper and behave irrationally. When you lose control of your temper, you stop thinking clearly and may make mistakes. Self-control also applies to self-defense. Not all self-defense means fear of serious injury. Sometimes the best self-defense is avoiding a fight, rather than trying to hurt your attacker. Self-control lets you think more clearly and make good decisions

Martial arts are a lifelong discipline and study. It is training that stays with you in everything you do. Martial arts are good for both physical and mental well-being. The *do* in tae kwon *do* or karate-*do* means *the way*. The way of martial arts is the way of life.

About the Authors

Mill Valley, California based karate and tae kwon do master, **Roger Carlon,** has been teaching martial arts for over 20 years at his West America Tae Kwon Do school. He is well known within the martial arts world for his expertise in teaching children, as well as adults.

Carlon is himself a national and international tournament champion, having won numerous grand championships in the United States, Canada, and Europe. His young students are also national champions, having won more medals than any other school in the 1998 Amateur Athlete Union National Tae Kwon Do Championships in Orlando, Florida.

Besides tae kwon do and karate, Carlon has extensive experience in hapkido, muay Thai, ju-jutsu, and Okinawan weaponry.

Carlon says there has been a tremendous increase in the number of children studying martial arts because kicking is so prevalent in action films.

"In the old days, you saw John Wayne punching, and now you see kicking. Children take kicking expertise as a challenge and they excel at it, because children tend to me more flexible than adults."

Jane Hallander may well be the best known and most prolific martial arts writer of all time. She has been writing about all segments of martial arts since the late 1970s. She has written hundreds of articles and numerous books. She is also a well-respected Chinese martial arts' instructor and tournament judge.